Praise for *The Co*
Book

'I've really enjoyed dipping in and out of *The Communication Book*, and found lots of really useful ideas and concepts that I either hadn't seen before or had totally forgotten about!

'I think that is where the real strength of this book lies, insofar as much of it is common sense stuff that when you read it you feel like you intuitively know it already, but with the constant distractions of home and work getting in our way every day, we quickly forget about the advice that Emma provides with such clarity.

'Giving feedback – especially when the message is a difficult one – can be something that strikes fear into the most experienced of managers, and Emma's book gives everyone a clear and concise guide on how to navigate these difficult waters with honesty and empathy.'

Georgina Farrell, Human Resources Director

'Emma Ledden is a proven expert in the field of communication and this is a must read for any aspiring executives looking to improve their professional communication skills.'

Gordon Tobin, Head of Global Sales University, LinkedIn

'Insightful, practical and easy to follow. Another great read by Emma Ledden. This book leads the charge on how to communicate effectively.'

Mairead Fleming, Managing Director, Brightwater Recruitment Specialists

'Emma's new book, *The Communication Book*, demonstrates that by using her techniques in their career search, readers will be able to clinch that next role by communicating their personal brand and selling themselves much more effectively to their chosen company.

'*The Communication Book* encapsulates all that is good about Emma's style and personality together with the passion she has for making you, the reader, the best you can be in communicating effectively with your chosen audience. The three-step approach in preparation before you speak is at the heart of it all.'

ne Manager,
iness School

'Emma perfectly captures communications in the corporate world and breaks them down into a series of straightforward steps, identifying the preparations and delivery techniques while covering the most common pitfalls that everyone makes. The cheat sheets she provides brilliantly and simply capture each section, and should have prime position on cubical and office walls. The book serves both the inexperienced/nervous communicator and as a great refresher to the more experienced executive.

'I particularly enjoyed the piece on building personal brands, something that is often overlooked as people look to accelerate their career. It's well structured and can be read cover to cover or as an on-going reference for specific situations.'

David Forde, Director of Sales Strategy,
EMEA at Salesforce.com

The
Communication
Book

The Communication Book

How to say it, mean it and make it matter

Emma Ledden

PEARSON

Harlow, England • London • New York • Boston • San Francisco • Toronto • Sydney
Auckland • Singapore • Hong Kong • Tokyo • Seoul • Taipei • New Delhi
Cape Town • São Paulo • Mexico City • Madrid • Amsterdam • Munich • Paris • Milan

PEARSON EDUCATION LIMITED
Edinburgh Gate
Harlow CM20 2JE
United Kingdom
Tel: +44 (0)1279 623623
Web: www.pearson.com/uk

First published 2014 (print and electronic)

Pearson Education is not responsible for the content of third-party internet sites.

ISBN: 978-1-292-06320-1 (print)
       978-1-292-06321-8 (eText)
       978-1-292-06322-5 (PDF)
       978-1-292-06323-2 (ePub)

British Library Cataloguing-in-Publication Data
A catalogue record for the print edition is available from the British Library

Library of Congress Cataloging-in-Publication Data
Ledden, Emma.
  The communication book : how to say it, mean it and make it matter / Emma Ledden.
    pages cm
  Includes index.
  ISBN 978-1-292-06320-1
  1. Communication in management. 2. Business communication. 3. Interpersonal communication. I. Title.
  HD30.3.L43 2014
  658.4'5--dc23
                              2014019864

10 9 8 7 6 5 4 3 2 1
18 17 16 15 14

Cover design by redeyoffdesign.com, cover image © yienkeat/Shutterstock.com

Print edition typeset in 9.5/13pt Mundo Sans Std by 3
Print edition printed and bound in Great Britain by Ashford Colour Press, Gosport
NOTE THAT ANY PAGE CROSS REFERENCES REFER TO THE PRINT EDITION

The Communication Book promise

This book will show you how to prepare and deliver a great piece of verbal communication instantly and simply for the most important scenarios you face in business today.

CONTENTS

ABOUT THE AUTHOR

Emma is an international presentation and communication specialist, speaker and author. During her career to date she has done it all – MTV VJ, BBC TV presenter, radio host, business woman and author.

Emma began her career presenting for Ireland's National Broadcaster (RTE), producing and presenting her own slot for two and a half years.

Following this, Emma was chosen from over 2,000 hopefuls to become a VJ for MTV U.K. This involved being in front of a television camera five days a week.

Here, she presented *The Dancefloor Chart Show*, *Select*, *Weekend Edition* and *MTV News*. Within six months Emma landed another very high-profile television position. She was chosen to present BBC's flagship programme *Live and Kicking*.

During this time Emma fronted major ad campaigns including Pepsi and Lee Jeans as well as gracing the front covers and pages of international magazines including *Maxim*, *Ministry*, *Loaded*, *Heat*, *FHM* and *Company*. Emma has interviewed some of the world's biggest stars, including Posh and Becks, Kylie Minogue, Robbie Williams, The Spice Girls, Justin Timberlake, Gwen Stefani, The Rock, Britney, Take That and Beyoncé.

Emma also worked in radio for a number of years as a producer and presenter. First she worked on a weekend magazine programme and then she progressed to producing and presenting a breakfast programme. Emma still contributes to the media regularly and is a recurring panellist and presenter on radio and television.

Today, Emma is a leading international Learning and Development, Presentation and Communication Skills specialist. For more information, please visit www.emmaledden.net.

Emma published her first book, *The Presentation Book*, in September 2013.

ACKNOWLEDGEMENTS

I would like to thank Eloise Cook and Pearson for the opportunity to write another book. I would like to thank Lucy Carter, Paul East, Emma Devlin and the Pearson creative team for their support and work. I would like to thank Susan McMahon and Ed Fidgeon-Kavanagh for their talents and time. I couldn't have done it without you all. Thank you.

Publisher's acknowledgements

The publisher would like to thank the following for their kind permission to reproduce their photographs:

Shutterstock.com: yienkeat front cover; ollyy pages 5 and 40; Sarah Cheriton-Jones pages 15(t), 34, 136 and 140; rangizzz pages 15(b) and 34; auremar page 19; Levent Konuk page 22; iofoto page 23; Elnur page 28; alexmillos page 30; Blaj Gabriel page 43; Felix Mizioznikov page 52; Fuzz-Bones page 53(t); wavebreakmedia page 53(b); Ljupco Smokovski page 63; Helga Esteb page 68(t); DFree page 68(b); vipflash page 69; Minerva Studio page 82; ChrisMilesPhoto page 84; bikeriderlondon pages 88 and 159; carrie-nelson pages 95, 96 and 112; Paul Vasarhelyi page 102; Florin Stana page 137; Dalibor Sevaljevic page 145; ala737 page 146; Aaron Amat pages 158 and 175; StudioFI page 171; R.legosyn page 177.

All other images © Pearson Education.

We are also grateful to the following for permission to reproduce copyright material:

Killer questions text on pages 109–10 from www.linkedin.com/today/post/article/20130123154152-201849-32-killer-interview-questions, reproduced courtesy of Aaron Hurst.

ACKNOWLEDGEMENTS

In some instances we have been unable to trace the owners of copyright material, and we would appreciate any information that would enable us to do so. We apologise in advance for any unintentional omissions. We would be pleased to insert the appropriate acknowledgement in any subsequent edition of this publication.

INTRODUCTION

In the hierarchy of communication, face-to-face verbal communication is no. 1. Face-to-face verbal communication is the most effective and impactful way you have to connect, engage and influence.

Ninety per cent of the success of your verbal communication is determined before you speak.

The number-one reason why verbal communication fails every day is a lack of skill on the part of the speaker.

The skill of verbal communication is one very few people have the opportunity to master, and for many it feels like something just out of reach. Here's the good news – effective verbal communication is not a case of pot luck, personality or genetics. Communication is a skill that can be acquired through preparation, patience, practice and the right approach.

The right approach

Our working day is a series of interactions; it is said we have 170 on average each day. You have these exchanges in offices, boardrooms and over the phone. You converse with people you know and people you don't know, people who connect with you, people who lecture you and people you would rather not have to talk to at all, I imagine.

These exchanges are essential to your business relationships, career success and a positive daily experience. At the centre of these interactions are your verbal communication skills.

Verbal communication skills are the oxygen of relationships and the heart of career and business success. Yet all too often they fail. But why?

- Why do some people spend 30 minutes making small talk with you while others barely say hello?

- Why do some people give you their full attention while others won't even make eye contact when you walk into their office?

- Why do some people speak to you with no regard for your feelings while others empathise fully?

Why is there not a simple, black-and-white answer to all this?

Because people are people – them, you and I.

We are humans talking to humans, and we must prepare for that fact. We must prepare to navigate the grey that is two different people with two different agendas, trying to get their needs met. We must remember there is no right or wrong.

We all see the world through our own unique, coloured glasses. We filter incoming information through our individual belief system, grounded in our exclusive experiences.

Great communicators understand and prepare for this. They have an approach they follow before they speak. They do not leave their communication success to chance.

To be a successful verbal communicator you must follow three simple steps.

1. Know the purpose

Your goal when you attend a job interview is very different to when you are at a networking event. The purpose of a team meeting is very different to the point of a media appearance. Technically, these interactions fall under the heading of communication, but they are very different in their purpose.

The first step to being an effective verbal communicator is to understand the purpose of the communication you are getting involved in, what you want and what you can realistically achieve.

2. Understand your listener

The only absolute in communication is that you are dealing with another human being. The only constant is that they will be inconsistent. The only security is the uncertainty of dealing with another person, their emotions and views.

Great communicators take the time to understand their listener.

THE VITAL QUESTIONS TO ASK YOURSELF

- What does your listener know, think and feel before you start talking?
- What do you want them to know, think and feel when you are finished?

It is vital you take the time to understand the person you have to interact with before you speak.

3. Prepare to speak

You know how it goes, don't you? You plan what you are going to say, in your head. You're crystal clear, in your head. You know your stuff, in your head.

Then you speak.

The result: 'That sounded so much better in my head'.

Whether you are talking to someone one to one or to a group, you must plan what you are going to say and even practise out loud how you are going to say it, so you can have flow and clarity.

The Communication Book takes this very simple, practical and unique three-step approach and applies it to the following scenarios: one-to-one conversations, giving feedback, networking, job interviews, facilitation and being interviewed by the media.

For each of these six business scenarios, the three steps will be explored fully and a 'cheat sheet' summarising the main tips will be at the end of each chapter.

At the heart of this book is the three-step approach in practice, with an explanation and one-page templates you can use to help you prepare for success in whichever scenario you find yourself.

Finally, *The Communication Book* also gives tools and techniques to improve your personal brand and non-verbal communication.

This book will show you how to prepare and deliver a great piece of verbal communication instantly and simply for the most important scenarios you face in business today.

The rest is up to you.

Section 1

Communicating to build relationships

Communicating one to one

STEP 1
Know the purpose

What is your communication goal?

Every interaction you have is going to be different, but your best chance of success is to understand the vital part you play in your communication. You can't just talk, focus only on your own agenda, have no clear point and expect the listener to do all the work.

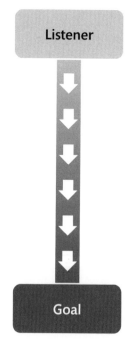

The first step to being a great communicator is to take responsibility for the experience you are creating when you speak. To be a great communicator you must do three things:

1. *Engage the listener:* tell them why they should listen.

2. *Take the listener through your information in the most relevant, understandable and enjoyable way:* yes, I do mean enjoyable.

3. *Ensure you achieve your communication goal:* you must have a communication goal.

We communicate every single day to:

- give information;

- express our emotions;

- provide advice;

- deliver feedback;

- sell our product or service;

- influence;

- motivate;

- educate.

Too often, the communication doesn't achieve its goal and fails. More often than not, we open our mouths and words come tumbling out. The right words, the wrong words and everything in between. Words we hadn't planned, words we didn't mean and sometimes words we wish we could take back.

We open our mouth and we talk. And it is the talking that gets us into trouble.

The trouble with talking

Words have a great power. Every time you speak you have the potential to build or un-build a relationship.

It is for this reason you need to:

- plan your words;

- place your words in the right order;

- make sure the words you are speaking are relevant and understandable to the listener.

You also need to plan to pause, plan to listen and plan what questions you will ask.

Finally, you need to plan for the unexpected – plan to manage your emotion and plan for the worst-case scenario.

Phew! That is a lot of planning, I know. I love planning (seriously, I do), but I realise this is not a universal feeling so let me change the word 'plan' for you in the hope of making this as easy as possible.

Think. You simply need to think before you talk. That's it.

Most people's approach to verbal communication is to talk without thinking. You must change this fundamental approach if it is yours. You must stop and think before you speak.

You must move from simply speaking in a freestyle manner, with no consideration for your words or their impact, and begin to prepare your communication, your everyday business interactions, in a listener-focused way.

What does this look like?

The *talking approach* to communication happens when the speaker:

- does not take the time to understand the listener and how to connect with them;

- does not prepare clear messages;
- assumes the listener is listening and understands;
- talks when it is too late or at the wrong time;
- is not prepared to manage difficult conversations.

Listener-focused communication happens when the speaker:

- understands the listener: they find out how much or how little the listener knows or understands about the message or interaction before it happens and they start from there;
- knows what they want to say: the speaker identifies the central point or points they want to communicate;
- has a clear structure and has their points in the right order;
- is prepared to deal with questions and accepts people will need to ask questions to clarify for themselves what they understand;
- is saying the right words, in the right way, at the right time.

It is your communication. You must own it. Be clear on the purpose, the point and the path before you speak.

> 'Handle words with care. They may damage you as well as others.'
>
> **TASNEEM HAMEED**

STEP 2
Know your listener

Great communication is an active process that involves engagement, energy and movement.

The purpose of great communication is to get your listener from one point to another in the best possible way. To do this you must:

- engage the listener;

- take the listener through your information in the most relevant, under-standable and enjoyable way;

- ensure you achieve your communication goal.

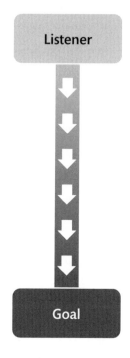

To achieve this you must consider your listener and how you are going to connect with them.

You can do this in three ways:

1. profiling them;

2. making sure they are floating;

3. giving them a reason to listen.

Stage 1: profile your listener

One of my favourite shows on television at the moment is called *Criminal Minds*. It is about a special team of FBI profilers who analyse criminals to determine their next move so that they can catch them.

They begin by understanding all they can about the criminal. They look at their past behaviour, emotions and circumstances to figure out how they will behave in the future. They gather as much information as they can about the criminal. This is the art of profiling someone.

Profiling is about understanding someone, how they think and what is important to them. To be a great communicator you must profile your listener before you speak.

You must gain an understanding of where they are coming from, what your communication will mean to them and how they might react to it, before you speak.

Profiling is about getting into someone's head, standing in their shoes and understanding where your listener is at before you speak.

Stage 2: make sure they are floating

Your listeners will always fall into one of three categories:

- the converted;
- the unconvertible;
- the floater.

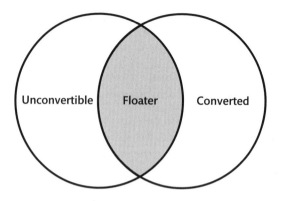

The converted

This is someone who is already doing, thinking or feeling the things you want them to before you speak.

The converted may feature in business scenarios like these:

- A fellow team member is at a meeting where you are giving an update on the progress of the project. They are in the room during the meeting but they are not the person/people you are trying to communicate with as they already know the project status, because they work on the project with you.

- You might be going for a job interview and your manager is one member of the interview panel. Your manager knows you and your work and may have decided you are the right person for the job before the interview. This person is the converted, so there is no persuasion necessary.

- You may be at a networking event and a friend introduces you to a new connection and you begin discussing what you do for a living. This information is given to educate your new acquaintance. Your friend knows what you do and is, as such, the converted in this scenario.

The converted may be present when you communicate but they are not your primary listener.

The unconvertible

When your listener is in this position they can't be converted.

'We were on a break!'

As well as *Criminal Minds*, I also watch re-runs of *Friends* on TV. If you do too you will know Ross and Rachel and their on-again/off-again relationship in the sitcom.

On one of their most memorable breaks, Ross went off with another woman. Rachel saw this as a betrayal because they only broke up for one night. Ross maintained they were 'on a break' and he did not betray her.

This was to become a recurring fight as, despite Rachel trying to convince Ross otherwise, he stood firm right to the end that he did nothing wrong as they were 'on a break'.

Ross is an example of the unconvertible (as is Rachel). No matter what anyone said, they both held their positions.

If we look at our business scenarios from the unconvertible position, this is what they look like:

- Work colleagues are at a department meeting where you are giving a project update. They work on a totally different project and your information has no impact or relevance to them. There is simply no reason for them to listen and they are not interested. They are in the room but not listening.

- You go for a job interview and a member of the interview panel believes another candidate of their choosing is more suitable for the job. They may ask you questions and listen to your answers, but for this individual, rightly or wrongly, their mind is made up so persuasion is impossible.

- You may be at a networking event and a friend introduces you to a new connection. This person has no interest in you. Maybe they are a bad networker, maybe they are just there to sell their service or maybe they don't care. Whatever the reason, you will never get to convert this new person as they are not open to the communication.

You will come across unconvertibles in your work life. The usual reason they are unconvertible is because your information has no impact on them whatsoever at that time.

The key message I want to deliver to you on this is: when someone is in this unconvertible position in relation to your communication, it means they cannot be converted at this time on this topic.

You may still deliver your messages and give them your information. They may listen and understand, yet still not do what you hoped. They may not listen to you at all.

You can give your information to an unconvertible but you can't expect them to convert.

The floater

The floaters are the group open to being communicated with, and your aim is to turn them into the converted.

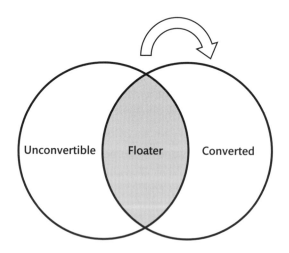

A floater will listen to you. A floater will engage with you. A floater can be converted, convinced and changed.

But... there is a 'but'.

You still have to do the work to make the movement from floater to converted happen. You must figure out why the person is still floating and what information they need to be converted.

Let's look at our scenarios one more time:

- You are at a department meeting giving an update and this update needs to be understood and actioned on by some people in the room. Your information has a huge impact on them but they do not know this. To move them from floater to converted you need to get their attention and let them know this status update is relevant for them.

- You are going for a job interview and there are some panel members who have no favoured candidate and will choose the person who communicates successfully. To convert these floaters you must prove you are the right person for the job.

- You are networking and meeting people who are interested in making connections. They are open to learning about you. To convert them you must tell them a little about what you do in this first meeting, keeping in mind your only purpose at this stage is to get a second meeting. Turning a floater to a converted is getting another meeting in this scenario.

To convert your floater you must give them more information or explain to them what they don't understand. You must figure out what questions they have about your topic, before you speak, and you must answer them as simply and clearly as possible.

Stage 3: give your listener a reason to listen

Any listener you ever find yourself in front of will listen to you for three reasons only:

1. They are sincerely interested in what you have to say.

2. They will gain something of value or they will benefit if they listen.

3. They fear they will lose something of value or there will be a negative consequence for them if they don't listen.

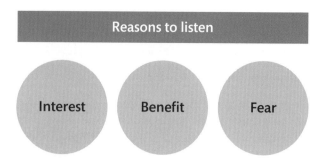

Probably the biggest mistake I see made by the people I work with is that they speak assuming they have the interest of the listener.

They guess, often wrongly, that the listener knows the relevance and importance of the information to be communicated. They assume the listener is genuinely interested. They protest that the listener *should* be interested.

Maybe the listener will listen, maybe they won't. Maybe they should, maybe they shouldn't. Maybe they know the importance of the message, maybe they don't. The truth is, you really have no idea or control if you rely on interest alone. So don't.

Don't place the burden on the listener to listen. Instead place it on you, the speaker, to give the reason to listen.

Your listener will only listen to you if there is a reason for them to listen.

If that is not genuine interest on their part, you, the speaker, must provide the reason to listen in the form of a benefit (gain) or negative consequence (loss) if the listener doesn't listen.

When you are about to communicate in any situation, the person you are talking to has two simple questions in their mind:

- How long will this last for?

- What's in it for me?

In other words... **Why should I listen?**

W.I.F.M?

Hooking your listener in

Listeners decide if something is worth listening to very quickly: they decide if they care about your communication in the first 45 seconds.

45
seconds

You must tell you listener clearly and simply in the first 45 seconds why they should listen to you. You must tell them why your information is of value to them or tell them the gain or the loss for them. You must do this in the first 45 seconds of your communication so you can hook them into the conversation.

Communicating the wrong way around

Many people do not prepare for their day-to-day interactions. As a result they speak off the cuff. Talking off the cuff can lead to a style of communication where you give a lot of background information and general facts before you actually get to the point you are making. By many listeners this is judged as waffling or rambling. Some, and I mean some, of this background information may be helpful or relevant but it is probably still in the wrong place.

The theoretical term for giving background information and reversing your way into your key point is *deductive reasoning*.

This means talking from the general to the more specific:

- beginning with general information and background;

- covering all possible areas related to the topic and going off on tangents;

- finally, right at the end, if the speaker has not confused themselves or everyone else, they will actually get to the point of the communication.

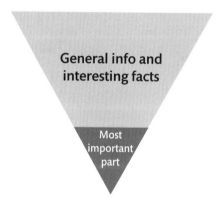

Deductive reasoning is a very legitimate approach to communication, but you really must ask yourself if your listener is going to wait until the end to get what they need. Would you wait?

I believe the answer is *sometimes*. Sometimes you will have a listener who does not mind this approach and is happy or willing to listen to the detailed background. I also believe there are many listeners who just want you to get to the point and get to the point fast. There are many who feel their precious time is being wasted when you use this approach. There are also many listeners who don't even know why they should be listening to you in the first place. For this reason it is essential to hook them in at the beginning by telling them the relevance and value of your information before you go into detail.

If you wish to engage a listener and get their attention, you need to turn the triangle the right way around.

Turn it the right side up

This is what is called *inductive reasoning*. Inductive reasoning moves from the specific to the more general yet relevant material. You must start with your most relevant and engaging point for your listener at the beginning. You can then go into detail explaining your point and backing it up for your listener.

This way the listener knows why they are listening and what's in it for them from the start.

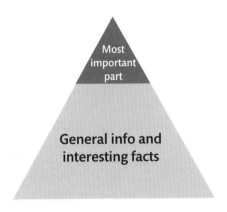

This is a great start. This is the right start.

Now you have their attention.

Now you have a chance.

Empathy – the essential element

We see the world not as it is but as it is for us. Our view of the world can be as unique as our finger print.

We can only see the world from the part of the window we are looking out from and this can be different for all of us. A vital element of great communication is to try and see the world through someone else's part of the window, as well as our own.

Why?

Because communication, at its very core, by its very definition, is about creating understanding and being understood. In order to do this we must be able to empathise. We must work to see with another's eyes, hear with another's ears and feel with another's heart.

EMPATHY

This is the ability to understand what others might be feeling and thinking. It is the ability to view the world through another person's eyes.

If you behave in an empathetic way towards someone, what you are doing is validating them. It says to another person that you have heard what they said, you see them and understand their viewpoint.

When you fail to empathise, you are failing to validate another person's view from their window.

This means you are actually rejecting the person you are speaking to. Not empathising when someone speaks is like putting your hand over their mouth when they are talking. Real connection is therefore impossible.

'Empathy fuels connection. Sympathy drives disconnection.'

DR BRENE BROWN

Empathising does not mean you agree or disagree. It simply means you see, hear, feel and understand how it is for someone else.

EMPATHY IS NOT THE SAME AS SYMPATHY

Sympathy is feeling *for*: sympathy and empathy are both acts of feeling, but with sympathy you feel for the person – you're sorry for them or pity them, but you don't specifically understand *what* they're feeling.

Empathy is feeling *with*: empathy is feeling with the person. It means you have a good sense of what they feel and you understand their feelings as far as is possible.

Sympathy is acknowledging there is another part of the window that someone might look through, but empathy is actually being able to see the world through that window pane.

One of the ways you can display empathy is through active listening, which we will explore in our next section.

STEP 3
Prepare to speak

Our everyday interactions involve three elements:

- Speaking
- Questioning
- Listening

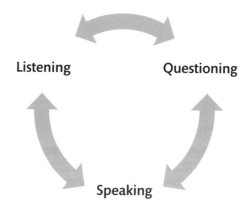

Listening   **Questioning**

Speaking

These three elements are woven together inextricably to make up our daily conversations.

I would like to take each element and give you some insight into the skills of speaking, questioning and listening.

Speaking

Speaking is the part where you have something to say – a message to deliver or a story to tell.

Most people I work with tell me they are not good at delivering a point or message, because they:

- waffle;

- can't get to the point;

- are not clear themselves what they are talking about.

The truth is, too often this self-diagnosis is correct. I continually meet individuals who make the mistakes listed above.

The good news is, there is a very simple reason why they can't deliver a clear point or message: they are not preparing a clear point before they speak.

I am going to repeat that again as it is very important.

You can't deliver a clear point if you haven't prepared one... and preparing in your head doesn't count.

Mulling it over in your head, believing you know what you are going to say in your mind, will never materialise into clear, concise spoken communication. There are many different ways to say things, and that is why the words you speak may be different to how you planned to speak in your head.

> **'Everything becomes a little different as soon as it is spoken out loud.'**
>
> **HERMANN HESSE**

If you don't prepare relevant and structured verbal communication, you will end up subjecting your listener to what I call the **'all you can speak buffet'**. Have you been to a restaurant or event where a buffet meal was served?

It's where there is every possible variety of food available and you must go with your plate and pick the food you want and leave the food you don't want.

In communication terms, the 'all you can speak buffet' is giving lots of information when you speak (some relevant and some not so relevant) and expecting your listener to pick and choose what points they want and what points they don't.

You are expecting your listener to pick and choose from all the information you are offering.

The 'all you can speak buffet' involves a lot of work on the part of your listener to sort through your words.

The question: Is your listener willing to work that hard?

I don't believe they are. They want you to do the work for them. They want you to serve them up tailored, relevant messages.

What if, instead of the 'all you can speak buffet', you treated your listener to **'Michelin-star communication'**?

A Michelin star is awarded to select restaurants globally, based on the excellent overall experience they deliver to their customers. Michelin-star restaurants serve the finest food, in bite-size portions, that flow from one course to another creating a pleasurable overall experience.

I want you to start preparing Michelin-star communication, where you:

- pre-select and tailor your information based on the listener's needs;

- deliver your points clearly;

- do all the work and allow your listener to sit and enjoy the experience.

You can do this by following the '**communication rule of three**'.

In order to give your listener clear points and tailored information you will need to decide what your key points are before you speak. If you have lots of information, you will need to organise or package this information into groups so that your information is digestible and memorable for the listener. One of the most effective ways to do this is by following the 'communication rule of three'.

Communication rule of three

The 'communication rule of three' is a very general rule in speaking, writing and music that says ideas presented in threes are inherently more interesting, more understandable and more memorable.

Stories have a beginning, middle and end. Many movies and books are works of trilogy.

There are many famous speeches and taglines that follow this rule, for example: 'Work, rest and play', 'Life, liberty and the pursuit of happiness', 'Stop, look and listen'.

In order to give your audience Michelin-star communication you must examine your information and ask yourself, what are my three key points?. If you have a lot of information to deliver, you must group all this information into three key areas – like a story with a beginning, middle and end section.

Questioning

Questions are a vital part of our communication tool kit. We ask questions to:

- get information;
- clarify;
- understand an issue;
- show interest;
- build rapport.

There are four main question types you need to be most aware of:

1. Open questions.

2. Probing questions.

3. Mirroring questions.

4. Closed questions.

Open questions

These questions get you started. They are general, information-gathering questions to which there is no right or wrong answer.

These questions usually begin with the words 'what', 'where', 'why' or 'how'. For example:

- *'Where do you see solutions...?'*

- *'What do you think of the idea...?'*

- *'Which is the best way to tackle the problem of...?'*

These are the best types of questions for getting a conversation started. They are thought-provoking and elicit a variety of possible answers. These questions are used to start a discussion and to get the ball rolling.

Probing questions

These questions pick up on the main issues (usually from a response to the open question) and move the discussion further along. They are the *'tell me more'* questions. They allow an issue to be probed into in more detail. You ask the person to tell you more about the issue.

Mirroring questions

These types of questions check for understanding, as the issue is being discussed in detail. A mirroring question uses the other person's words to confirm that they really meant what they said.

Closed questions

These questions always produce a 'Yes' or 'No' answer. They are very useful in summing up and confirming actions at the end of an interaction.

The funnel effect

Good questioning is about using these four question types to get to and gain a proper understanding of the underlying information, the real need or the heart of an issue.

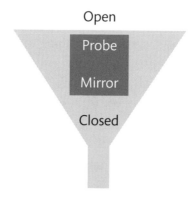

There are three steps involved in 'the funnel effect':

1. **Open questions:** Always start with open questions about the subject. This will give you all the information you need to take the conversation further.

2. **Probing and mirroring questions:** This stage of the questioning will allow you to delve deeper into the listener's answers, finding out the reasons and emotions behind those answers.

3. **Closed questions:** Asking closed questions allows you to confirm both your and the other person's **understanding** of what has been discussed. It will also show the listener you have been listening.

THE FUNNEL IN ACTION

Let's look at an example of the funnel effect in action.

Louise just went in to see her boss, Alan, to ask for two weeks off work. Let's see how she got on:

Open question
'What happened with Alan when you went into his office to ask for two weeks off?'

Probing questions
'What is the first thing you said to him?'
'How did he react?'
'Were you surprised by his reaction?'

Mirroring question
'You felt very shocked and a little disappointed about his refusal to give you the time off?'

Closed question
'So you don't have the full two weeks off, but he has agreed to give you a week off?'

A question of quality

You have no control over how someone responds to your questions, but there are things you can do to help the questioning process run more smoothly.

- Prepare each question before you ask it. Do not develop the question while you are asking it.

- Make your questions as concise as possible.

- Do not ramble, go off on a tangent or give irrelevant information in the middle of your question.

- Ask only one question at a time.

- Avoid asking multiple choice questions, such as 'When you were travelling to work today did you take the train, the bus or a taxi?'. Just ask, 'How did you travel to work today?'.

- Phrase questions simply, using everyday language.

- Maintain eye contact with your listener while asking questions and listening to responses.

- Ask your question then stop talking and wait for the answer. You need to allow a reasonable amount of time for your listener to consider the question and come up with their answer. A common mistake we all make is to expect an immediate reply. When it doesn't come we jump in too quickly with another question.

Silence is golden

You need to try hard to develop the ability to ask a good concise question, and then keep quiet.

If you are feeling nervous or impatient then a short silence can feel like an eternity, but if you fill silences too quickly you will seriously damage your ability to have good conversations.

It may help to visualise your question as a ball that you have thrown to the other person. When you have thrown the ball by asking a good, clear question, be silent. Don't say anything else until they have answered your question and thrown the ball back.

And if you are the one being asked the questions:

- *Listen carefully* to the whole question. People sometimes have a tendency to think they know the question and they stop listening before it has been asked in full. The completed question can be very different from what you predicted.

- *Show respect* to the person asking the question by looking at him or her and paying attention.

- *Never show signs of impatience or interrupt anyone*, even if they are asking a rambling or wordy question.

- *Nod your head agreeably* from time to time to encourage the person who may be having difficulty asking their question or being clear.

Listening

I have to admit something to you. I am an interrupter.

Sometimes I do it because I am too impatient to wait for the other person to get their entire answer out. Sometimes I interrupt because I think I know what the other person is going to say (because I am clairvoyant, you know). Most of the time I do it because something the other person said has triggered something in my head that I have to say straight away or I will burst!

Barriers to listening

Our daily working lives contain a bombardment of information from multiple sources and an uncountable number of distractions within and beyond our control. It can be very hard to be a good listener while battling the tsunami of daily data we face.

Some of the biggest barriers to being a good listener are:

- our beliefs and attitudes;

- a lack of interest;

- distractions.

Types of listening

There are three main ways you can listen in your everyday interactions;

- **Passive listening:** You are there physically, making eye contact but offering little or no feedback – verbal or non-verbal. This can result in the other person feeling you are not interested in the conversation.

- **Selective listening:** This is where you will 'tune out' of bits of the conversation. You will look disinterested, be easily distracted or will jump in to change the subject at the earliest opportunity. This can result in the other person feeling you have more interesting things going on elsewhere.

- **Active listening:** There are no shortcuts to becoming a great listener, and the price tag for poor listening is high. Listening well can cut down on misunderstandings, missed opportunities and disagreements. Listening well will build strong unions, increase knowledge and deliver better results.

Both of the first two listening styles can have a negative impact on your objectives of building and deepening relationships with your colleagues and clients. You need to be self-aware and try to not let yourself slip into these modes. To show interest, empathise and build good relationships you must listen actively.

Real listening is an *active* not *passive* process. You have to choose to give your undivided attention.

How to become an active listener:

1. Be present:

- Give your full attention to the speaker.
- Don't interact with your phone while someone is talking to you.
- If you can't give your full attention, reschedule.

2. Wait your turn:

- Don't talk before the speaker has finished.
- Recognise how impolite it is to interrupt the speaker.

3. Listen non-verbally:

- Be aware of body language – both your own and the person you are speaking to. Face the speaker fully and maintain good eye contact.
- Use verbal and non-verbal signals to confirm you are paying attention (e.g. nodding or shaking your head and verbal expressions such as 'Yes' or 'No').
- Smile (when appropriate).

4. Pause:

- Wait a few seconds and absorb the information before responding.

5. Empathise and be honest:

- Seek to understand what is being said.
- Don't pretend you understand – if you are not sure, repeat what you think is being said in your own words.

ASSUMPTION – THE ACHILLES HEEL OF COMMUNICATION

Quiz time!

I want you to elect a new world leader, and your vote counts.

Here are the facts about the three leading candidates:

- **Candidate A**: Associates with crooked politicians and consults with astrologists. He's had two mistresses. He also chain smokes and drinks 8–10 martinis a day.

- **Candidate B**: He was kicked out of office twice, sleeps until noon, used heroin in college and drinks a bottle of whisky every evening.

- **Candidate C**: He's a decorated war hero. He's a vegetarian, doesn't smoke, drinks an occasional beer and hasn't had any extramarital affairs.

Who do you choose as your world leader?

We all make decisions and judgements based on the information we have. And often we make decisions in assessing whether something is right or wrong before seeking the full story.

Without the full story, without asking the right questions and listening to the answers fully, we can make bad judgements that, in turn, cause bad decisions.

Make sure you have the full story before you make a decision. Why?

Here are your world leader candidates' names:

- **Candidate A**: Franklin D. Roosevelt

- **Candidate B**: Winston Churchill

- **Candidate C**: Adolph Hitler

...I voted for Hitler, too.

What's in it for you?

When our daily interactions fail it is very easy to focus on and blame the elements we have no control over, as there are many. It's more comfortable to look at others and see how they are communicating badly. It's effortless to accuse someone else of being difficult rather than putting our own behaviours and attitudes under a microscope and asking questions such as:

- Did I have a clear communication goal?

- Did I listen?

- Did I try to understand?

Ultimately, this is about you getting what you need from your communication. This is possible if you take responsibility for your communication, understand your listener and prepare to speak.

Chapter cheat sheet

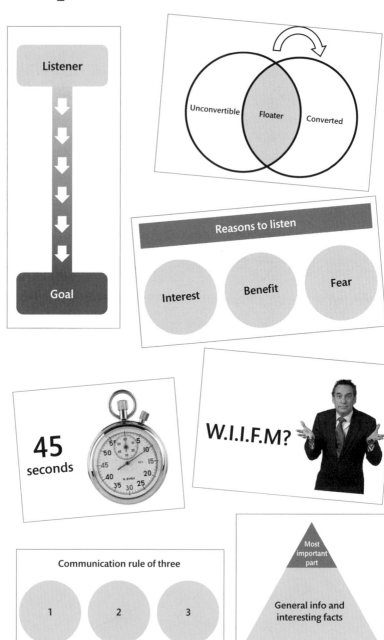

Communicating to give feedback

STEP 1
Know the purpose

According to a survey from the L.E.A.D (Leadership, Employment and Direction) survey book by the LMA (Leadership Management Australia), 'Today's workplace – Present realities... Future realities' (2013), the most important leadership attributes, in numerical order, are:

1. A good communicator who can provide feedback

2. Honest, trustworthy, ethical and fair

3. Understanding and a good listener

4. Compassionate, empathic and caring

5. Knowledgeable, competent and able to multi-task.

The need for feedback

When you manage or supervise people, it is your responsibility to give them feedback on their behaviour – both positive and negative. A lot of people shy away from giving feedback, especially negative feedback, as they do not want to cause offence or upset.

When you are giving people feedback you are trying to improve their ability to do their job successfully. Sometimes you do this by pointing out what they are doing well (a positive behaviour) so they can continue to do this. Other times you need to point out what wasn't done so well (a negative behaviour) so they can change it.

Types of feedback

Positive	Negative
• To recognise/reward and reinforce a specific behaviour	• To change a behaviour • To improve performance

I have never met a person who minds giving positive feedback.

However, negative (or developmental) feedback is a whole other ball game. Nobody likes giving that. It is such an awkward, uncomfortable conversation to have for everyone involved. You have no idea how the person will react to the negative feedback or if it will affect your relationship with them in the long term.

There are very genuine challenges when giving negative feedback. They include:

- giving feedback to someone in work whom you consider a friend as well as a colleague;

- not wanting to appear overly tough;

- not finding the right words to say;

- fearing a bad reaction;

- it's uncomfortable for everyone involved.

Unfortunately, because of these real obstacles, the speaker's goal is often just to get it over and done with as quickly as possible. Very often the person giving the feedback gives a vague, general, mixed-message-type feedback in the hope of not hurting the other person's feelings. The conversation then turns into a very negative experience for both people.

Do we really need to give negative feedback?

If it is so uncomfortable for everyone involved, why do we have to give it at all? I mean, if it's going to upset the other person maybe it's best not to say anything?

I am afraid Jo and Harry would disagree.

In the 1950s American psychologists Joseph Luft and Harry Ingham developed a concept called the 'Johari Window', and this concept explains why we must give and receive feedback.

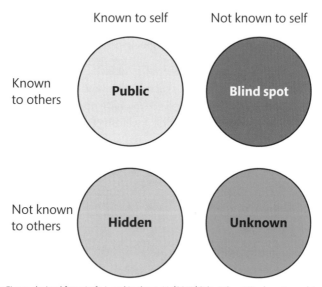

Source: Figure derived from Luft, J. and Ingham, H. (1955) 'The Johari Window: A graphic model of interpersonal awareness', proceedings of the Western Training Laboratory in Group Development. LA: UCLA Extension Office.

The idea behind the Johari Window is that we all have four selves, or sides, and each of these sides is either known or unknown to us or to others:

1. **Public**: something you know about yourself and that others know about you too.

2. **Hidden**: something you know about yourself but others do not know it about you.

3. **Unknown**: something you don't know about yourself and others don't know either (a hidden talent).

4. **Blind spot**: something you don't know about yourself but others know it, see it and are impacted by it, possibly in a negative way.

We must give and receive feedback because of our blind spot.

The blind spot is what is unknown by the person about him/herself but which others know. The person doesn't see it themselves but others see it and are impacted by it.

We must be told of any behaviour, positive or negative, we are not aware of that is impacting others because it will ultimately impact on us and our ability to be successful in our careers.

STEP 2
Understand your listener

Surprise!

Because most of the time the feedback we receive is in our blind spot, it tends to come as a surprise to us.

A good surprise – we are told of strengths we are not aware of that others admire.

A bad surprise – we are told a behaviour of ours is negatively impacting other people and causing them to view us in a negative light.

How feedback feels

Receiving feedback triggers us emotionally; therefore it must be emotionally processed. This emotional process is often referred to as **SARA** (**S**hock, **A**nger, **R**esistance, **A**cceptance).

1. **Shock:** This is probably genuinely brand-new information to the listener. Keeping in mind that the feedback is based on something in someone's blind spot, the first reaction they are going to have is shock – especially if what they hear is unexpected or contradicts their own view of themselves. When people are experiencing shock, they may say things like, 'What? I don't understand'.

2. **Anger:** As the listener realises what the feedback means, shock can turn into anger. At that moment the person receiving the feedback feels very exposed and uncertain. During the anger stage, people may say things like, 'Who said this anyway?'.

3. **Resistance:** If feedback indicates the need for change, the listener may experience a period of resistance. Change can be difficult, or at least uncomfortable. Resistance is where they explain, blame and excuse.

They brush off, deny and condemn. In truth, they do anything and everything to resist the change. When experiencing resistance, people may say, 'That's just the way I am, take it or leave it', or 'That's just my personality, they are too sensitive'.

4. Acceptance: Finally, as the listener processes the feedback, they come to a point of acceptance, which leaves them at a better, more aware place than where they started. When an individual is finally accepting their feedback, you may hear them say, 'What can I do to improve?' or 'How can I best use this feedback?'.

People need to go through these four stages before they are able to use the feedback effectively to make improvements in their lives.

SARA: a typical reaction to a difficult message

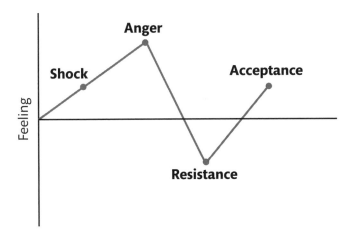

Straight to acceptance

Critical or unexpected feedback can leave someone in shock, feeling angry and possibly resistant to change for days, weeks, or longer.

The problem is, as the person giving the feedback, you want acceptance straight away. You don't want someone processing their shock, anger or resistance with you. It's uncomfortable to watch someone go through those emotions.

You must allow the person you are giving feedback to to have these feelings. They are allowed to be shocked, angry and even resistant. They are allowed to look for explanation and understanding. That is all they are doing.

The tightrope of empathy and authority you must walk as the speaker in this interaction is difficult to master. If your feedback has proper evidence behind it you should be able to move someone from shock to acceptance. If your feedback is vague, general and without evidence, then your listener may get stuck in one of the phases longer then you hoped.

The goal of good feedback is to try and move someone through this SARA process as easily as possible.

Let's look at how you do this.

STEP 3
Prepare to speak

This is Philip. He is a newly appointed manager in a consulting firm. Up until now he has been working very hard, but since being promoted he seems to have changed his attitude and is distracted. He has not been paying attention at meetings and has been called a bad listener by many of his fellow team members.

He is now having a meeting with his manager to be given feedback.

This is how the conversation goes:

'Hi Philip. I am here to give you some feedback I have received from the team. You have been very distracted lately, you are not listening at meetings and you need to pull your sock ups and pay more attention. OK? Thanks Philip.'

How do you think Philip is feeling?

Shocked, angry, resistant? Do you think Philip will accept this feedback straight away?

There is a good chance Philip won't accept it because the problem with this feedback is it is too general and Philip could easily go into shock, anger or resistance, protesting his innocence or annoyance.

Philip may also feel his whole character is being attacked. Phillip feels he works very hard and it is unfair to get this feedback.

To ensure Philip changes his behaviour in future meetings, the feedback will need to be given in a step-by-step way that Philip can understand and digest. Also, the feedback will need to be far more specific and behaviour-based.

A feedback framework

There are many models of feedback. The one I would like to introduce you to is the **EEC** feedback model. This model is very simple and effective and applies to giving both positive and negative feedback.

EEC stands for:

- Event
- Effect
- Change/Continue

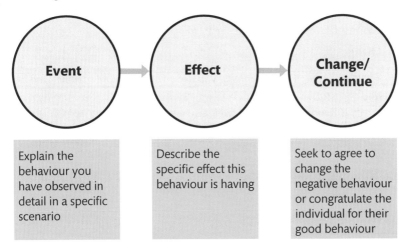

Event	Effect	Change/Continue
Explain the behaviour you have observed in detail in a specific scenario	Describe the specific effect this behaviour is having	Seek to agree to change the negative behaviour or congratulate the individual for their good behaviour

Let's go back to Philip and see how the feedback conversation would go if the EEC feedback model was used. The manager begins:

'Hi Philip. How are you? Is your current project going well and on target? How do you find working with the current team?'

From this the manager learns that Philip feels his current team leader is a bit domineering but he likes the team in general. He is very busy and wants to ensure the client is always happy. He has also told his manager he has a personal issue he is dealing with, but he doesn't wish to talk about it today.

Armed with this information, the manager continues:

Event

'Philip, you are a very valuable team member and we are very happy with how you have been working with the client. However, for the past four team meetings you have arrived between 15 and 30 minutes late, you have not prepared your update in advance (including not using the proper templates) and when your other team members are speaking you are on your blackberry the whole time. Are you aware of this?'

Effect

'This behaviour is having an impact on your team and on the meetings. You are overrunning on your time slot to speak, meaning other people have to rush their own update or the meeting runs over. Also, being on your phone shows a level of disinterest and disrespect to the other speakers at the meeting. Can you see that from the team's point of view?'

Change

'Philip, as I said at the beginning, you are a valuable team member and we would like to support you in every way we can. Do you agree, from here on in, you will commit to arriving on time to every team meeting, preparing your update fully, and finally can you please commit to not bringing your phone into the meeting? Thanks Philip.'

The facts about feedback

Giving and receiving feedback is a vital skill in your communication tool-kit. It is not an easy conversation, and that is why you must be ready for it.

You do, of course, have to give the feedback no matter what, so don't shy away from it at the last minute. Be clear, calm and confident in your information and empathetic yet assertive in your attitude. Remember the purpose of feedback is to help and support someone's career development. Feedback is a good thing, no matter how uncomfortable it may feel.

FEEDBACK NEEDS TO:

- **Be at the right time:** give feedback as close to the event as possible.

- **Ask them for their story first:** ask them what happened and let them tell their story.

- **Be behaviour-related:** focus on visible actions and behaviours, not general character traits. Give specific examples during your feedback.

- **Explain the impact:** explain the impact that their actions and behaviour had on the team, the client or the work.

- **Check for clear understanding:** check they understand the feedback. Also ensure you understand their viewpoint.

- **Discuss future solutions:** ensure they know what actions and behaviours you expect in the future.

If you are the one on the receiving end of feedback, remember you are likely to experience SARA. Here are a few things to remember:

1. Don't take it personally – make sure you focus on the facts.

2. Ask lots of questions to make sure you understand.

3. Don't make excuses – listen to understand.

4. Make sure your self-image stays positive.

5. Focus on the future and what you can improve.

What's in it for you?

Giving negative feedback is a difficult interaction for everyone. It is going to generate an emotional response in the other person, no matter how well it is done. Accept this.

If you have people who work for you it is your responsibility to make them aware of their blind spots – both the positive and negative behaviours they are not aware of.

My best advice is to make it about them as much as possible, rather than making it about you. Give good solid examples of the behaviour, give them a chance to speak first and, most importantly, allow them to feel their way through it.

Chapter cheat sheet

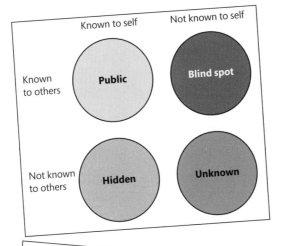

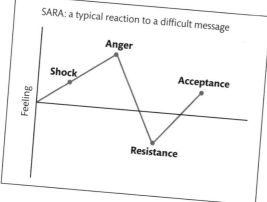

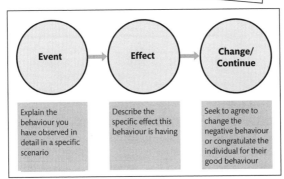

Communicating without words

I would like to introduce you to Dr Mehrabian.

Well not him so much as his famous communication model. This is it:

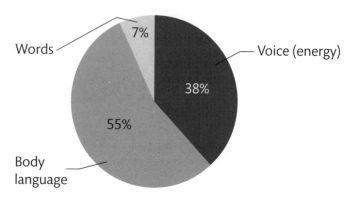

Source: Figure based on data from Mehrabian, A. (1981) *Silent messages: Implicit communication of emotions and attitudes*, Belmont, CA: Wadsworth.

This communication model claims when people are listening to you talk they judge you first by your body language, then by your voice and finally they judge what you say.

Let me start by saying this model does not mean your words or what you say are not important.

What this model is saying is that if your body language and voice (energy) are not saying the same things as your words, people will believe what your body language is saying first, then your voice and then your words.

For example, if you say you are really excited about something but speak these words in a quiet, monotone voice, looking at the floor and slumped over, people will have a hard time believing you are excited because you don't look or sound excited.

Words + Body Language + Voice = *Communication Success*

Words – Body Language – Voice = *Failed Communication*

Body language is a silent language, but it speaks louder than words. What this means is that your everyday exchanges and communication are made up of your verbal (speaking and questioning) and non-verbal communication (how you look and behave).

So let's look closely at the elements that make up your non-verbal communication. These include:

- how you *look*;

- how you *sound*;

- how you *feel*.

The great news is that all of the factors that make up your non-verbal communication are under your control.

How you look

Eye contact

Eye contact is one of the first things a listener notices about you. Having poor eye contact causes many problems in communication:

- **Poor connection**: you can't establish connection with a listener if you don't look at them.

- **No feedback**: you can't get or give feedback to a listener if you don't look at them.

- **Look of nervousness**: if you don't make eye contact, at best you look nervous and at worst you look untrustworthy. This means the listener may question your credibility.

The solution to these problems is to establish deliberate eye contact with your listener. If you are talking to more than one person, make eye contact with each of them one at a time for approximately three seconds each. However, if one of them asks you a question, focus more on them while answering it. Equally, if one person is talking, make eye contact with them more while they are speaking.

Body language – two wrongs and a right

There are three ways your body language can be judged by your listener – passive, aggressive or assertive.

1. PASSIVE BODY LANGUAGE

How you look:

- slumped;

- your shoulders are forward;

- you shift repeatedly from one foot to another;

- your chin is down.

You sound:

- quiet;

- full of hesitations such as 'em', 'ah' or 'um';

- nervous.

2. AGGRESSIVE BODY LANGUAGE

How you look:

- tense/rigid;
- your chin is up or thrust forward;
- your hands are clenched, or pointing;
- you have sweeping arms;
- you give sharp, quick nods;
- you rapidly tap your pencil (like a drumstick) while listening.

How you sound:

- you have a loud, harsh voice;
- your statements sound like orders;
- overconfident.

3. ASSERTIVE BODY LANGUAGE

How you look:

- upright/straight;
- you lean forward while listening;
- you use casual hand movements;
- you have relaxed hands;
- you occasionally nod your head.

You sound:

- firm/pleasant;
- prepared/calm;
- energetic/passionate.

Look the business

When I was a teenager I wanted to be taller so I could be a model. I am only 5ft 6 and I wanted to be 5ft 9 at least. Believing this (my height) was the only thing standing in the way of my career as the next supermodel, I went on a quest to be taller. I just needed 3 inches; surely I could get them from somewhere.

PLAN A

I started with the basics – really, really, really high shoes. This was a terrible plan. They were extremely uncomfortable. I looked ridiculous walking in them, and at every single model casting I went to, they asked me to take my shoes off. Nooooo!!!

PLAN B

Late one night, while channel surfing, I discovered a product on one of those home shopping channels that promised, through exercise, to make you taller. Jackpot!

Apparently, it was going to grow the muscle between my spine to make me taller. It made absolutely no sense to me either, but hey, I was going to be taller.

You may not be shocked to learn I am still waiting for my 'grow-taller exercises' product to arrive in the post.

I never did manage to be the next supermodel but, in my quest to be taller, and indeed as a TV presenter in the years that followed, I did see and experience the power of dressing for success and, more importantly, dressing for confidence.

I believe dressing appropriately is vital. No, it can't *make* you taller (trust me), or more beautiful, or change the fundamentals of who you are. However, it can make you *look* taller, feel more attractive, boost your self-confidence and help you make the right impression on those you meet.

Here are a few basics rules everyone should follow.

1. Personal hygiene is important. You need to shower, you need to brush your teeth and you need to wear deodorant. Your clothes need to be clean and fresh and if you smoke, please be aware of how that smell impacts other people.

2. Be careful you don't overdo the perfume or aftershave.

3. Your hair should be clean and groomed (my secret weapon to feeling more confident is a blow-dry).

4. Dress for the industry you are in and as your listener would expect.

5. Wear clothes that fit you properly, nether too big nor too small.

6. Please don't go to work dressed as though you are going to a night club (unless, of course, you work in a nightclub).

7. Wearing black tights does not equal more skirt length; your skirt needs to be to the knee if you work in a corporate environment.

8. Do not flash your underwear or cleavage at work, no matter how nice either or both are. Please see point number 6.

9. If in doubt, be a bit more conservative than you think you should.

10. Buy the best quality clothing you can afford.

How you sound

> **THREE ELEMENTS TO BE AWARE OF**
>
> 1. **Posture**: speaking is a physical act. Stand up straight and tall, place your weight comfortably on both feet and create a strong resonance chamber for your voice. If seated, sit up straight and plant your feet on the ground.
>
>   **Position**: face the listener completely and don't cover your mouth when you are talking.
>
>   **Passion**: if you don't genuinely feel passion and enthusiasm, this will come across in your voice.

Passion

Passion is an essential ingredient for your voice to be impactful.

Passion simply means you care about what you are talking about – you believe in your subject and getting to the communication goal.

Passion is the opposite of indifference. If you feel your message is boring and irrelevant, then this is how you are going to make the listener feel. You must be convinced of your message before anyone else can be.

HOW PASSION SHOWS UP IN YOUR VOICE

In natural speech, our voice range varies naturally between high and low throughout a conversation. However, sometimes due to nerves or lack of interest, people have little variation when they speak.

An additional problem with a lack of passion is that the speaker usually comes across looking unenergetic.

Your personal energy level has a major influence on the person you are talking to – either matching their energy level, raising it, or bringing it down.

We are all different. Whether you are naturally lively and outgoing, or innately thoughtful and reserved, you will definitely have a 'range' of energy levels. Get to know your personal 'default' level, and try to practise turning that default level up a notch or two and down a notch or two.

It's important to have a good understanding of yourself and how you might need to 'turn the energy up or down' when you are communicating.

The power of the pause

When you are speaking it is very natural to talk through your information quickly. People talk fast due to nerves, lack of awareness or lack of preparation.

One of the most powerful communication tools available to you as a speaker is the pause.

A pause is when you stop talking, you take a breath in and then a breath out. It should last about three seconds, but those three seconds can feel like three hours. We all have an enormous urge to fill up every single second of the silence with our voice. Silence in a room can be very overwhelming for any speaker, especially in front of a group.

You must pause:

- for your listener to digest your messages;
- so you, the speaker, can breathe.

You need to embrace, plan and practise your pausing.

Most speakers don't talk too fast, they simply don't allow any space between their key points.

- You need to pause *at the beginning* of your communication, before you start speaking, to make sure the listener is ready to listen.

- You need to pause either *before or after* you make an important point.

- You need to pause when you *give a hand-out or put up a slide* to allow people to take it in.

How you feel

There are three common feelings that come up consistently for the people with whom I work:

- lack of confidence;
- nerves;
- being emotionally triggered.

Lack of confidence

I don't have a magic solution to this obstacle. In my mind it is very simple: we feel confident about the things in our life we are skilled at. We are skilled at them because we work hard at them and have earned the right to feel confident.

To have confidence you must have experience of doing something a lot and belief you can do it without making a fool of yourself (this comes from the experience).

Confidence is not acquired easily and you don't get it for free.

There is no short cut to real confidence. The reasons you don't feel confident are:

- you lack the experience (the skill of communication);

- you are not preparing properly, or enough (you have not earned the right to feel confident).

The four steps to building your confidence as a communicator are:

1. Do an honest inventory of your communication skills by asking for feedback.

2. Look for opportunities to practise and get experience.

3. Allow yourself a degree of failure in your interactions; you are not perfect.

4. Ensure you reflect and learn from your mistakes.

Get more experience to build the skill and do more preparation and you will feel more confident in your exchanges.

> 'Inaction breeds doubt and fear. Action breeds confidence and courage. If you want to conquer fear, do not sit at home and think about it. Go out and get busy.'
>
> DALE CARNEGIE

Nerves

It can happen when you least expect it. It can happen when you are utterly unprepared and, annoyingly, when you have put hours of planning into your communication.

It can be a feeling – heart racing, stomach churning, head pounding, dizziness – not visible to the naked eye, but very overwhelming for the person experiencing it.

It can be a blushing that starts at your chest and runs the whole way up your neck and face. A physical shaking of your hands, legs or voice. It can be a fidgeting of hair, hands, clothes and anything else within arm's length. These are the visible signs you are feeling anxious.

We all experience it and would pay anyone any amount of money to make it stop, make it go away.

What am I talking about? *Feeling nervous, of course.*

HERE COMES THE SCIENCE...

Anxiety or nervousness is the body's way of responding to being in a life-or-death situation. *What!* How is talking to someone a life-or-death situation?

Even in our everyday interactions we fear embarrassing ourselves, fear we will be found out, fear we are not enough. You know that feeling, don't you?

It is this very genuine ego fear that we all share, this 'I will die of embarrassment if I make a fool of myself' belief that triggers our fight-or-flight response. When this survival mechanism is triggered in our bodies it causes the feelings of nerves to hit us suddenly, unexpectedly and without mercy.

Embarrassing yourself in front of someone important is perceived as life or death for your ego, and that is why the feelings you get are so strong and real.

When this fight-or-flight response is triggered, adrenaline is rushed into your bloodstream to enable you to run away from or fight the dangerous situation.

This happens whether the danger is real, or whether we believe the danger is there when actually there is none.

What this simply means is your internal survival system can't tell the difference between a real life-and-death situation and a communication scenario (where you might embarrass yourself).

The first step to managing your nerves is recognising this response and why it is happening. Your body is just telling you this is important and you don't want to mess it up.

The behaviours that happen when you feel nervous are:

- self-talk/inner critic;
- avoiding eye contact with the listener;
- moving from foot to foot;
- talking fast;
- general fidgeting.

These behaviours help you cope with anxiety and yet they will take away from your messages and your communication goal.

I can't tell you how to get rid of nerves, as this is not possible. Your goal is not to get rid of, but to accept and manage your nerves so they don't overwhelm you. There are only two ways I know how to manage nerves. They are:

1. Prepare fully.

2. Mentally support yourself.

Ninety per cent of the success of your communication is in the preparation before you speak. You must use the tools in this book to know your purpose, understand your listener and prepare your words. You must practise out loud and ensure you know what you are going to say and how you are going to say it. You must do all this before you are in the real-life situation.

When the day comes and you are in the business scenario for real, you must try and calm yourself down and mentally cope with your nerves. You must challenge your inner critic and feel confident in the preparation work you have done.

Stop! Pause, take a breath and don't react automatically to your feelings.

Ask yourself:

- What am I reacting to?

- What is it that I think is going to happen here?

- Is this fact or opinion?

- Am I getting things out of proportion?

- How important is this really? How important will it be in six months' time?

- Am I overestimating the danger?

- Am I underestimating my ability to cope?

- Am I mind-reading what others might be thinking?

- What advice would I give someone else in this situation?

- Am I putting more pressure on myself?

- Just because I feel bad, does it mean things really are bad?

Being emotionally triggered

Imagine this scenario: you are interviewing for your dream job; you are prepared but are feeling a little insecure.

During the interview you have a feeling one of the people on the panel doesn't really like you. You have no evidence of this. He hasn't done anything specific, but it's the way he looks at you. He seems bored by your answers and dismissive of your experience. At least, that is how it feels for you.

Then it happens. This interviewer asks you the question you have been dreading, in a tone of voice you feel is very condescending *'Why should we choose you over the other candidates?'.*

That's what is said... but what you actually hear is *'You are not good enough for this job and I don't really like you'...*

And that is what is called emotionally responding to a question.

You might respond emotionally because:

- it could be a very reasonable question asked in an aggressive or dismissive tone;

- it could be a question you hadn't planned for and you feel under pressure to now give a perfect answer;

- it could be a question you simply don't know the answer to and you don't know how to handle it.

All of these situations have one thing in common. They will cause you to answer the question with emotion rather than fact. Why?

Because they have triggered your emotions: if someone asks you a question in a dismissive tone, it is normal to feel defensive or angry in return. If you feel you are going to be caught out, it is normal to go into self-survival mode and start scrambling for answers.

Finally, if you believe you should know everything, when the day comes when you are asked a question you don't know the answer to (and it will come), you will become overwhelmed. Instead of just admitting you don't know, you will react emotionally and show, through your emotions, that you don't know.

When you are interacting with someone, questions can be asked in a way that causes an emotional reaction in you.

Stop! Do not answer the emotion part of the question, answer the fact part.

Respond to the data part of the question being asked and not the emotion it triggers in you.

Let's go back to our condescending interviewer. He simply asked 'Why should we choose you over the other candidates?'. This is a very reasonable question at a job interview. Maybe he did ask it in a patronising way, maybe that is how he talks, maybe he is nervous asking the question, maybe he doesn't like you.

The truth is you simply don't know, so be careful not to assume the worst. Be careful not to bring all your past emotional baggage into this new scenario.

WHEN ASKED AN EMOTIVE QUESTION YOU MUST:

- pause and breathe;
- not take the tone personally but manage your own emotion as best you can;
- ask them to repeat the question;
- be clear on what facts they want;
- answer the fact or data part of the question.

We are all guilty of responding to a situation today with the feelings of yesterday.

Section 2

Communicating to build your career

Communicating your personal brand

What are the first words that come into your mind when you think of Richard Branson?

How about the first words that come into your mind when you think of Oprah Winfrey?

And finally what are the first words that come into your mind when you think of Lady Gaga?

Now, what if I put your picture here?

- What words would you use to describe yourself?

- What words would your team use to describe you?

- What words would your manager/superior use to describe you?

Would the words be the same for all three? Would they be the right words? Would they be the words you want used to describe you?

That is a lot of questions. Let me start at the beginning.

It's a brand new world

The term 'personal brand' is believed to have first appeared in the August 1997 issue of *Fast Company Magazine*, in an article by Tom Peters.

Tom said that we live in the age of the individual. Our working life no longer involves going into one company at 18 years old and working until retirement, safe in the knowledge that time served, rather than suitability, will ensure career progression.

Today, in a world of enormous ambition and fortuitous competition, there is little job security. Careers are created and changed yearly, and the rein-vention and expansion of self is vital for success. This is why your personal brand is worth your attention.

Each one of us needs to think of ourselves, brand ourselves and market our-selves as if we are a business such as Nike, Coke or Tommy Hilfiger. We need to be clear on what we are good at, what makes us different and we need to be excited, no, really excited, about our brand before anyone else can be.

To succeed in business today you must be CEO of Me Inc. You have to decide what your personal brand is and then you need to show it to the world in everything you do – confidently and consistently.

This chapter will help you do that.

> 'It's this simple: You are a brand. You are in charge of your brand. There is no single path to success. And there is no one right way to create the brand called You. Except this: Start today. Or else.'
>
> TOM PETERS

Become CEO of Me Inc

I am not here to tell you what your personal brand is or should be.

You choose your own personal brand.

You know if you are Lady Gaga, Richard Branson, Hugh Hefner or Miley Cyrus.

The most important message I want you to get from this chapter is that you are always creating an impression, every day, in every interaction. I want you to be aware of that impression and I want you to be sure you are coming across the way you want and need for your career success.

You are a walking, talking personal brand, whether you like it or not. Today, right now, the way you dress, the way you talk, the way you interact – that is your personal brand. If you refuse to believe in personal brands, that belief is part of your personal brand. Everything you do and everything you choose not to do communicates your personal brand.

Some people I meet feel the idea of a personal brand is too contrived or engineered, but this is not about spin. Being aware of and having a genuine personal brand is not fake; it is simply knowing who you are, identifying your strengths and making sure that when you are out there in the world of work you are representing yourself correctly and honestly every day.

You can develop yourself and your skills as part of your personal brand. You may believe you are quite shy but would like to be known as a great speaker. In this case, you may choose to work on your presentation skills.

However, aside from building new skills, do not try to be something you are not. You will only be able to pretend to be somebody else for so long before you show the world truly who you are.

Who are you?

We live in an age where few people have or want a job for life. We live in this incredibly exciting time where we can be and do anything we want.

If only it was that easy though. Yes, maybe we can be and do anything we want, but to achieve that we must know ourselves, represent ourselves and, in a lot of cases, stand out from others.

There is much written about personal branding, but I believe it is very simply the act of knowing yourself and being who you are, consistently and professionally.

There are three simple steps to identifying and communicating your personal brand:

- **Awareness**: do a personal brand audit.
- **A-list**: pick your words.
- **Action**: put your words into action with the '7 Personal Branding Basics'.

Awareness

The first step to identifying your true personal brand is to do a **personal brand audit**. This exercise will help you identify and become aware of what your personal brand is today.

There are three parts to this exercise.

What three words would you use to describe yourself?

1.

2.

3.

What three words would a work peer use to describe you?

1.

2.

3.

What three words would your manager/superior use to describe you?

1.

2.

3.

You will need to ask your work colleagues and your manager to fill this out. You are looking at your personal brand in work, rather than in your personal life. Some people are different in work than they are in their private life. That is OK. I am sure Lady Gaga doesn't go around wearing those crazy outfits on a day off.

A-list

This is the fun part: now you get to pick your ideal words, the words you want people to use to describe you. The goal is to get absolute clarity on who you are and what is unique and amazing about you. Remember to be authentic and keep in mind the feedback you got in your audit. Start by circling any words at all that appeal to you and then edit them until you have six words in total.

Accepting	Authentic	Chic
Accomplished	Authoritative	Child-like
Achievement	Awake	Clever
Adorable	Aware	Comfort
Adventurous	Big picture	Compassionate
Affectionate	Bohemian	Connected
Ambition	Bookish	Conservative
Ambitious	Brave	Controlling
Angelic	Calm	Cool
Appreciative	Canny	Cosmopolitan
Appropriate	Capable	Courage
Articulate	Captivate	Crazy
Artistic	Careful	Creative
Attentive	Caring	Credible
Attract	Catalyst	Cuddly
Attractive	Cheap	Cute

Cynical	Empathetic	Perky
Dad	Encourage	Perseverance
Dapper	Energise	Persuasive
Daring	Enlightened	Playful
Dark	Entertaining	Prepared
Dedicated	Experienced	Real
Dependable	Fun	Rebellious
Detail-orientated	Funky	Relaxed
Determined	Glamour	Reserved
Devoted	Grace	Responsible
Diamond in the rough	Humorous	Risk-avoiding
Diligent	Inspirational	Rule-breaker
Direct	Integrity	Rule-follower
Discerning	Intelligent	Sensible
Distinguished	International	Sensitive
Diva	Joyful	Serene
Down to earth	Kind	Sexy
Dramatic	Mum	Silly
Earthy	Non-judgemental	Simplicity
Eclectic	Non-traditional	Sincere
Educated	Open-minded	Smart
Effective	Optimistic	Sporty
Efficient	Original	Strong
Elegant	Party animal	Stylish
Emotional	Perceptive	Subtle

Successful   Traditional   Trustworthy

Sultry   Transformative

Sunny   Trendy

Action

At this stage you have examined and received feedback on your current personal brand and you have chosen the six words you want to be known for, based on the list I gave you.

Now you must figure out how you are going to communicate your brand (those six words) every day in the ways that matter.

Below are the '7 personal branding basics' you need to think about.

1. YOUR VOICEMAIL MESSAGE

Do you use the phone company voice message? Do you record a simple 'I am not available to take your call now' message? Do you update it every day and say what you are doing or how available you are? Do you leave a funny message to music? What best represents your personal brand?

2. YOUR EMAIL SIGNATURE

'Kind regards', 'Yours sincerely', 'Cheers', 'Thanks', 'Merci', 'Grazie', 'Faleminderit' (that's thank you in Albanian you know... gotta love Google) are all options for your email signature.

Do you put all your social media contacts and website details at the end of your email? And what about a photo? What best represents your personal brand?

3. YOUR LINKEDIN PROFILE

Are you on LinkedIn? Maybe you are half on it, thinking about going on it or just not sure what to do with it. If you are going to be on it, make sure it represents you properly.

If you need help with this there are great YouTube videos and blogs, and the site itself can help you maximise your profile.

4. YOUR CONTENT

Your emails, proposals and presentations are all a representation of you. You need to make sure they are prepared, spell-checked and on time at the very least.

5. YOUR BUSINESS CARD

Do you need one? If so, it needs to be of good quality. Use both sides and have the right contact details on it. Feel proud handing out your business card and make sure it represents you and your brand.

6. YOUR CLOTHES

I talked about dress in an earlier chapter, along with the importance of being groomed. But dressing for your personal brand is more than that. Dressing for your personal brand is about making a statement with your clothes. It is about saying you are a leader or you are creative or you are non-traditional. It could be the tie or tights you wear. It could be the shoes or the suit. It could be the lipstick or lapels you choose.

A CareerBuilder.com survey reports that 41 per cent of employers state that people who dress better or more professionally tend to be promoted more often than others in their organisation.

Financial services is one of the industries that places the most emphasis on professional dress, as 55 per cent state that people who dress more professionally tend to be promoted more often than others in the organisation. On the other hand, IT and manufacturing are two of the industries that place the least amount of emphasis on professional dress, as only 37 per cent and 34 per cent, respectively, said that employees who dress more professionally tend to be promoted more often than others.

'Even though we are seeing a trend of more relaxed dress codes in the office, especially in summer, it doesn't mean that professionalism should go out the window', said Rosemary Haefner, vice president of human resources for CareerBuilder.com. 'How you dress can play an important role in how others perceive you at work, and dressing professionally can help you project a motivated and dedicated image.'

Haefner recommends the following tips for dressing professionally on the job:

- **Stock your wardrobe**: start with the versatile basics, such as a pair of black trousers, a dark trouser suit, some button-down collared shirts and a classic pair of dark shoes. Once you have the staples, you can continue to build your wardrobe to give you plenty of professional options.

- **Keep it neat and clean**: make sure your trousers, shirts and other clothes are ironed, stain-free and in good condition. When your clothes look sloppy, so do you.

- **Steer clear of bar attire**: don't mistake the office for your local watering hole. Leave the slinky shirts, tight trousers and cut-off t-shirts at home.

- **Look the part**: if you have a client presentation or a meeting with the CEO then dress for the part, making sure you choose appropriate articles of clothing for your role.

The way you dress matters and says so much about you. Make sure you are saying the right thing.

7. YOUR ATTITUDE

Your attitude is visible to everyone.

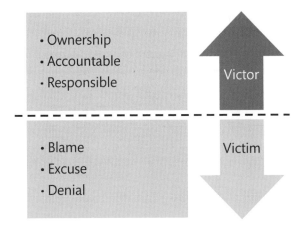

Do you smile or sigh in your everyday interactions? Are you open or insular? Are you stressed or stable? Do you yell and scream at your laptop when it won't work (me too sometimes) or do you calmly joke of the joys of technology and how precious it is?

You need to ensure your attitude is above the line, as indicated in the diagram on the previous page, so that you are a victor not a victim. You need to approach each day and each exchange with an attitude of ownership, accountability and responsibility.

Everyday etiquette

There is one final area we need to look at under the heading of personal branding and it is what I call 'everyday etiquette'.

It is up to you to decide to consciously work on your personal brand, but what you do need to be sure you are aware of, every day, is how you are treating other people.

Respect is a behaviour you must display in every interaction. Respect is visible in the things you do. Respect is turning off your phone to listen to someone, not interrupting when someone is speaking and not making the conversation about you all the time.

> **'I must respect the opinions of others even if I disagree with them.'**
>
> **HERBERT H. LEHMAN**

As human beings we all have the right to be treated with respect. We have the right to express our feelings and opinions. We have the right to be listened to and taken seriously. We have the right to make a mistake and change our mind. We have the right to ask for what we need, as long as we accept that asking does not necessarily mean we will get it.

In our everyday interactions and explorations respect is displayed in the little things we do.

RULES OF EVERYDAY ETIQUETTE

- **Pleases and thank yous:** the oldies but still the goodies of modern manners.

- **Be on time:** being on time shows your respect for the other person. Don't be late, if you can help it. It's really rude and everyone else's time is just as valuable as yours.

- **Help others** if you see someone whose arms are overloaded with packages, open the door. If you have just entered a building and someone is right behind you, hold the door to keep it from slamming in his or her face.

- **Go quietly amid the noise and haste:** this world has become very noisy. Be careful not to add to it unnecessarily. Keep your mobile phone ringer-volume as low as possible. If you work in an office cubicle, be considerate of your fellow office mates by keeping your voice low while chatting on the phone.

- **Parking:** this one drives me crazy. Please don't park across two car park spaces just because they are both free.

Communicating
to network

STEP 1
Know the purpose

Hands up who loves networking? I don't have my hand up either.

Networking is like dating – emotionally exhausting, mentally draining and just when you think you've met the man of your dreams, he begins the date with the phrase – 'I Googled you'. (True story.)

Like dating, networking involves a series of awkward interactions where you must be pleasant, polite and make sure you don't do anything you will regret the next day.

Net**work**ing = work. So why bother networking? Well for the same reason we date: **connection**. We are trying to find 'our people'. Find our tribe. Our tribe will support us and help us move along in our career. Our tribe will become our clients, customers or maybe even our friends.

Meet Laura

I would like to introduce you to Laura. Laura attends many networking events, but doesn't seem to get what she needs from them. Laura is not really clear what she needs from her networking, but she soldiers on – spending more and more of her precious time networking.

This is typically the approach Laura takes to a networking event:

- Laura has no real aim or mission when she attends this event, she just has a vague notion of networking.

- The conference starts at 8.00pm and Laura arrives at 7.55pm.

- Laura runs straight to her comfort zone – the tea/coffee area.

- Laura then grabs onto the first person she knows, a friend of hers who is also attending the event.

- The bell rings and Laura goes in to listen to the presentations or have dinner.

- At dinner Laura speaks only to the people on either side of her.

- Laura waits for the acceptable time after dinner and then leaves.

- She jumps into a taxi and wakes up at 6am the next morning exhausted and feeling like networking is not working for her.

What is networking?

Networking is not about selling. Networking is not about instant gratification. Networking is not a one-night stand; it is the first encounter in what you hope will be a long-term relationship.

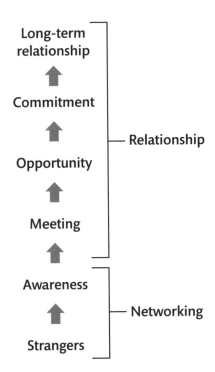

Networking is about meeting people – *new* people. It is about talking to people and seeing if you have a business-relationship future together.

The first step to great networking is to meet as many of the right people as you can, talk to them and see if you can get to know them better.

So what did Laura do wrong in her approach to networking?

Unfortunately, quite a lot.

STEP 2
Understand your listener

Now let me introduce you to Mark

Mark believes networking is very important and he is very good it at. Mark attends many networking events and is very clear on his networking objective and what he wants to achieve. Mark is married with two children so he can't be out all night, every night, networking.

This is how Mark approaches a typical networking event:

- Before he goes near the conference he identifies the three people he wants to meet and talk to.

- How? He calls the conference organiser and gets the list of attendees. Not an easy thing to achieve and he usually has to do some negotiation to get it.

- Once he has the list of attendees he picks the three people he wants to meet and does some research on them on the internet.

- Remember, Laura arrived at 7.55pm, grabbed a tea or coffee and headed into the presentation or dinner, speaking only to the people beside her. Mark does not do this. Mark arrives at the networking event 30 minutes early. Why? It means he can grab people as they come in. He doesn't have to break into existing groups.

- If he doesn't know what his target person looks like, he will ask the organiser to let him know when they come in. When he or she arrives he goes straight over, introduces himself, chats for a few minutes and then arranges to follow up in the most suitable way.

- How does he know what to say? He knew who he was meeting so he researched them a little and has a conversation-starter ready.

- By 7.55pm, if he chooses, Mark is able to go home when everyone else (including Laura) is going in to dinner.

WHAT MARK DOES IN MORE DETAIL

1. He has a clear networking goal to meet three people.
2. He gets the list of attendees in advance.
3. He does some research and prepares what to say to the people he wants to meet.
4. He proactively and confidently approaches his target people.
5. He keeps it simple, short and engaging, as his goal is to get a follow-up meeting, not to sell on the spot.

What if you can't get hold of the attendee list?

A huge part of Mark's success lies in his preparation and ability to get the attendee list. In most cases you should be able to do this but, if not:

- look at the speakers and the event and try to figure out which industries/people are likely to be there;

- on the day of the event, arrive early and ask the organiser for help identifying some key people to chat to;

- do your best to come up with an alternative strategy for meeting the right people before you attend, using your existing network and contacts.

OK, you are at the event and you have to talk to complete strangers. . . What do you do?

STEP 3
Prepare to speak

Working the room

In order to work the room at your networking event you need to be able to:

- break into existing groups;

- have an interesting conversation ready;

- move on when necessary.

Breaking into existing groups

If you are not able to grab people as they come in the door then you may need to break into existing groups of two or more people and join their conversation.

The first thing to remember is, it is a networking event and people are all there for the same reason. It is not helpful to have an 'I don't want to disturb them' mind-set when networking. Generally, people do not mind you joining them.

If in doubt about this, always take a moment or two to hover a little and get a sense of the conversation you are breaking into.

Once you feel ready, walk up confidently and say: 'Hi. Do you mind if I join you?'.

Having a conversation ready

If you are breaking into a group and want to begin a general conversation then:

- Talk about the event – have they been to it before and is it different to last year?

- Offer a story or anecdote or something of interest to the group.

If you are starting a conversation with an individual:

- Research them in advance as this will give you something to say; this is the ideal scenario.

- If you haven't been able to research them, say 'I simply wanted to put a name to the face. It is lovely to meet you, here is my business card. Could I give you a call sometime to talk with you in more detail about your company and the work you do?'

- The best networkers do less talking and more listening. Show an interest in the person you are talking to and ask questions. People love talking about themselves.

WHAT DO YOU DO?

The most common question you will be asked at any networking event is 'What do you do?'.

This question is an opportunity to explain to people what you do in a short time-frame and in a way that will leave them wanting more. A lot of people call the answer to this question their 'elevator pitch', the idea being, you have the time it takes to ride an elevator to tell someone what you do in an interesting and engaging way. The time suggested is 60 seconds.

Remember, the point of networking is to get a follow-up meeting and to start building a relationship. Elevator pitches should not involve any kind of selling. The goal is to say enough to gain the person's interest, so that they will want to know more.

QUESTIONS TO ASK WHEN CREATING YOUR ELEVATOR PITCH

- What service/product do I offer?
- What problem does it solve or need does it meet?
- How am I different?

Here are some examples of elevator pitches to give you a flavour of what yours might look like.

'You know how most business people use PowerPoint but don't know how to use it properly, which can lead to loss of sales or reputation? My company shows businesses how to create presentations and use PowerPoint to communicate their great ideas in the right way. We use a unique method we developed based on the techniques used on TV.'

'I consult time-challenged business owners on how to build teams and become more productive and profitable. I'm in a unique position to help my clients because I've faced the same struggles myself. I have figured out a formula that can help just about any entrepreneur build a team, giving them the time they need to grow their businesses.'

'My company develops mobile applications that businesses use to train their staff remotely across the globe. The approach we use is unique because we visit each organisation to find out exactly what their people need and then build applications to suit them from there.'

HOW DO I STOP PEOPLE BREAKING AWAY FROM ME?

Remember, it is a networking event and everyone you talk to has their own goals, so you can't monopolise their time. Don't be afraid of the conversation ending. Give your business card and ask if it's OK to follow up after the event.

While you are talking to someone you can do your best to keep them interested by asking them about themselves, talking about their business or any hobbies or current affairs topics you might share an interest in.

If you are going on and on about yourself they will want to run away.

Moving on when necessary

You will also want to move on from conversations to ensure you meet the three people you have planned for. Leaving a conversation politely and firmly is perfectly acceptable.

One way to do this is to say: 'There is Mary. I was really hoping to talk to her, so please excuse me. It was a pleasure to meet you. I will email you in the next week.'

The other alternative is to introduce someone else to the person you are talking to and then leave.

Following up

The event is over and you achieved your goal of meeting your three key people.

What happens next?

If the first encounter went well and you feel it is right to take the next step, then you must get in touch and arrange the most appropriate follow up.

There are many methods you can use to follow up and keep in touch:

- a compliment slip with a relevant newspaper article;
- an email;

- a telephone call;
- an invitation to an event or to see round your office;
- an invitation to lunch or coffee.

However, there is a chance you will get to this follow-up stage and, despite an offer to meet or take things further, the relationship won't develop. Part of good networking is recognising this and not letting it put you off future networking.

NETWORKING QUICK TIPS

- Don't get drunk.
- Don't talk about yourself the entire time.
- Listen actively.
- Have enough business cards with you.
- Avoid subjects that are inappropriate.

What's in it for you?

A strong network can be an enormous asset to you as you build your career.

Your network can act as your coach, your recruiter, your advocate, your mentor and your sounding board.

A good network can introduce you to the right people, tell you about an internal job opportunity or expose you to ideas and ways of working you didn't know existed.

Most importantly, your network knows you, supports you and values what you do.

Chapter cheat sheet

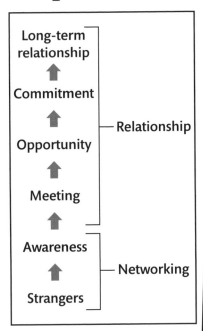

Long-term
relationship

⬆

Commitment

⬆

Opportunity — Relationship

⬆

Meeting

⬆

Awareness

⬆ — Networking

Strangers

Questions to ask when creating your elevator pitch:
- What service/product do I offer?
- What problem does it solve or need does it meet?
- How am I different?

What Mark does in more detail:
- He has a clear networking goal to meet three people.
- He gets the list of attendees in advance.
- He does some research and prepares what to say to the people he wants to meet.
- He proactively and confidently approaches his target people.
- He keeps it simple, short and engaging, as his goal is to get a follow-up meeting, not to sell on the spot.

There are many methods you can use to follow up and keep in touch:
- the compliment slip with a relevant newspaper article.
- an email.
- a telephone call.
- an invitation to an event or to see round your office.
- an invitation to lunch or coffee.

Communicating to get that job

STEP 1
Know the purpose

Job interviews are the one great equaliser among us. We all have to do them.

No matter our age, experience or background, they shake us to our very core. Who does not lie awake at night wondering how to answer *that* question: 'What is your biggest weakness?'. Aaaaaaaaaggghhhhh!

So let's start with the basics.

What is the job of a job interview?

The job of a job interview is to find the right person for the job.

You have 10 candidates who all want the job and all think they are the right person.

The job interview is the filtering process each candidate must go through.

These 10 candidates must prove they are the right person for the job. **The onus is on the candidate and not the interviewer.** This is not always an easy reality for candidates to face.

There are three major obstacles that must be overcome to do well in a job interview.

1. I deserve it

A lot of people who are preparing for a job interview feel they deserve the job and that it is unfair to have to interview to get it. They feel their years of service should speak for themselves.

Here's the thing. Maybe it's not fair. Maybe you do deserve the job. Maybe you have been doing the job for two years without the title, recognition or salary. Maybe... but that is not how the world works.

I am going to have to 'Dr Phil' you now. Are you ready...

Job interviews are a huge part of business life and career success.

You have to do them. You have to go into them with an attitude of fight and want. If you really are the right person for the job then it should be no problem for you to prove that to an interview panel.

Which leads me on to the second biggest issue.

2. I don't want to sell myself

Another very common statement made to me by people going for job interviews is 'I don't want to sell myself'.

They tell me: 'I don't feel comfortable talking about myself. I don't want to brag. I don't want to come across immodest. I don't want to be too pushy, arrogant or in-your-face.'

Over to you again Dr Phil...

THE WHOLE POINT OF A JOB INTERVIEW IS TO SELL YOURSELF

Selling yourself in a job interview does not mean:

- you lie or exaggerate;
- you make big statements you can't back up;
- you are loud and arrogant.

This is not about employing any dishonest car-salesman tactics, or pretending to be something you are not. Selling yourself at a job interview is not proclaiming how great you are in a boastful manner. It is about proving you are the right person for the role.

Selling yourself at a job interview is about:

- understanding the role and the skills needed;
- telling the interviewer that you have those skills;

- proving you have those skills by using real examples and evidence from your career.

You must be prepared to do this if you are to have any chance of job-interview success.

3. It's not an oral exam

Do you remember doing oral exams in school? You go into the room with the examiner, you sit glued to the chair, petrified, waiting. Waiting for the first question. Waiting for the next question. Waiting for the *right question*. The question you hope will come. The question you studied for. This is so often how people approach a job interview.

You can't take this passive approach to job interviews.

Job interviews are not oral exams and you are not 15 years old any more (thankfully).

Job interviews are a negotiation. The interviewer is coming to the table with a job – you must come with something too.

You must come with your skill set and with examples to back those skills up. You must come with enthusiasm and a want to communicate and negotiate. You must come to a job interview ready to prove you are the right person for the job.

To succeed at a job interview you must:

- look at the job spec and figure out what skills are needed;

- be honest about whether you have those skills;

- prepare examples from your career history to prove you have those skills.

A search for skills

The first step to prepare for a job interview is to figure out the skills required for the role. Some job specs spell the skills out for you and others are less clear.

Let's look at an example of a role for a project manager.

Description: project manager

Project manager job duties:

- Accomplishes human resource objectives by recruiting, selecting, orientating, training, assigning, scheduling, coaching, counselling and disciplining employees; communicating job expectations; planning, monitoring, appraising and reviewing job contributions; planning and reviewing compensation actions; enforcing policies and procedures.

- Achieves operational objectives by contributing information and recommendations to strategic plans and reviews; preparing and completing action plans; implementing production, productivity, quality and customer-service standards; resolving problems; completing audits; identifying trends; determining system improvements; implementing change.

- Meets financial objectives by forecasting requirements; preparing an annual budget; scheduling expenditures; analysing variances; initiating corrective actions.

- Updates job knowledge by participating in educational opportunities; reading professional publications; maintaining personal networks; participating in professional organisations.

So what skills are they looking for here?

Based on the job spec, I would say they are looking for:

- budget management;
- coaching;
- supervision;
- recruitment;
- project management;
- people management;
- process improvement;

- self-development;

- planning;

- performance management;

- verbal communication;

- leadership.

This list is a great starting place because once you are clear on the skills needed you just need to use those skills to answer the interview questions.

The other bit of good news is that a lot of jobs require similar professional skills, so it shouldn't be too hard to identify which skills are needed for any role.

Start by examining the job spec on offer. Then look at similar job specs on the internet to get more information if necessary.

Here is a list that covers most professional skills, to help you identify which skills you might need to talk about at your job interview:

Teamwork	Strategic thinking
Managing change	Technical expertise
Developing others	Initiative
Managing people	Innovation
Communication	Results-orientated
Influencing others	Decisiveness
Building relationships	Self-confidence
Customer focus	Stress management
Information gathering	Flexibility
Conceptual thinking	

> # STEP 2
> # Understand your listener

The person/people interviewing you is/are human

They have friends, a family, are overworked, underpaid and, believe it or not, they are just as stressed and nervous to be there as you are.

I train both interviewers and interviewees and I honestly believe the first group are more nervous than the latter.

Why? There are a few reasons:

1. **No training:** most interviewers I have met have never been trained to be an interviewer. It is a skill you need to learn and, without the tools to ask good questions or to listen effectively, it can feel very daunting.

2. **The choice:** interviewers have the power to choose one candidate over many others. In fact, this is their role and they do not take it lightly, in my experience. All job interviewers are aware of the choice they must make and how only one person can be chosen. They also must be able to stand by that choice if questioned on it.

3. **The cost of a bad hire:** they say it is better to make no hire than the wrong hire. Picking the wrong person at a job interview has enormous collateral costs, both on the culture and the bottom line of an organisation.

> ## THE OFFER
>
> Tony Hsieh, CEO of Zappos, has found a way to weed out employees who aren't fully committed right at the start.
>
> All new Zappos employees are greeted with a four-week training programme. At the end of the first week everyone is offered $2,000 to quit. The offer stands until the end of the fourth week. Zappos wants employees who really want to work for them, and no one else.

The role of the interviewer

The role of the interviewer is to find the right person for the job.

They do this by:

- understanding the key skills needed to perform the role;
- finding out if the candidate has the required skills by asking the right questions;
- assessing all this information and choosing the best candidate.

An interviewer's job is to get behind your CV and really examine the skills you possess.

The interviewer will look at certain things:

- Whether there are any gaps in the timeline of your CV.
- What the key events in your career are thus far.
- What your core skills are, based on your work to date.
- What you are like – education, hobbies and interests.

Criticisms of the candidate

Interviewers do not have an easy job, and the ones I have worked with say interview candidates can be their own worst enemies by:

- not preparing for the interview;
- not listening to the questions or answering the wrong question;
- providing irrelevant information;
- making negative comments about themselves, thus showing a lack of confidence;
- not taking opportunities to sell themselves;
- not showing enthusiasm or passion.

Be your own best interviewer

As interviewers are looking to get as much relevant information as possible, they will usually ask a series of leading questions.

An example of a leading question is:

Question: *'Give me an example of when you worked on a team?'*

Answer: *'I have a number of examples I could share with you. In one instance, when I was working at XYZ Company, the IT team was pulling together a bid for a large piece of work and the staff member that normally helps them out was on leave. I offered to help them and worked late every night for two weeks to ensure they had all the information they needed. As it turned out, we won the bid and I was promoted as a result.'*

But what if the interviewer doesn't ask a leading question, or is trying not to help you out too much? Then they may ask a more general question like this:

Question: *'Are you a good team player?'*

Answer: *'Yes, I am a good team player and have worked on lots of teams.'*

And you stop there. They asked a question and you answered it.

The problem here is the interviewer does not have the information they need now to assess you properly. I know it could be argued they didn't ask a good question, well at least not a leading one. But this is where it is over to you.

You need to be your own best interviewer. You need to imagine that every question the interviewer asks requires more detail and examples.

Question: *'Are you a good team player?'*

Answer: *'I love working as part of a team and yes, I believe I am a very good team player. I have a number of examples I could share with you to prove this. In one instance, when I was working at XYZ Company, the IT team was pulling together a bid for a large piece of work and the staff member that normally helps them out was on leave. I offered to help them and worked late every night for two weeks to ensure they had all the information they needed. As it turned out, we won the bid and I was promoted as a result.'*

The interviewer's role is to find out if you have the skills, knowledge and attitude that fit the job.

You must help them with this search. You can't rely on them to always ask the right questions.

> **No matter the question, you must always have the right answer.**

STEP 3
Prepare to speak

Having the right answers

There are three parts of a job interview you need to prepare for:

- the opening questions;

- the skills-based questions;
- the closing questions.

Opening questions

'TELL US ABOUT YOURSELF.'

This is normally the first question in a job interview and it can be the most dangerous.

Where do you start, where do you end, and how much do you say?

The first thing to know here is, although they may not say it, this question has a second part.

'Tell us about yourself, **in relation to this role**.'

When you are asked to talk about yourself at a job interview they are not looking for what you did last weekend, what your favourite colour is or any other information that may in any way distract from the fact you are the perfect person for this job.

The question 'Tell us about yourself' is your first opportunity to tell this interview panel you are the right person for the job. It is your first opportunity to show you understand the role, the skills required and to show your passion.

If we use our project-manager example from earlier, the answer might be something like:

'I have been a project manager now for 10 years, working on small teams with as few as 3 people, to multi-million pound projects with teams of 40 people. My biggest strengths are budgeting and coaching junior team members to deliver on-time and on-target. This is something I really enjoy doing. I have invested in my own self-development over the years, attending many courses on presentation and negotiation skills.

I believe these skills are vital in a project-manager role to communicate with the various groups.'

'WHY DO YOU WANT THIS JOB?'

I once did interview training with an 18-year-old guy, just out of school, going for a job as a bank clerk. He didn't want the job, but his parents told him he had to go for it.

In the training session I asked him why he wanted the job. He told me the bus stop to work was right outside his house so that was handy for him. I asked if that was the only reason he wanted the job. He said yes.

It is still, to date, the most honest answer I have ever heard to that question.

It is also completely the wrong answer.

When you go for a job there are, of course, many personal reasons you have for wanting the job. They may be money-, career- or transport-related. However, whatever your personal reasons for wanting a job, these are not relevant, or at least are not what you tell an interviewer. Once again there is a second part to the question that is unsaid. It is:

'Why do you want this job, **in relation to us**?'

It simply comes back to the WIIFM – the 'What's in it for me?' question.

The interview panel want to know what *they* will get out of hiring you.

Going back to our project-manager example, the answer might look something like this:

'*The reason I applied for this role is that I have always admired your work and I feel this particular project would be a great fit for my skills. I believe this project will need strong budgeting skills, which I have, and I also believe you will need specific expertise in the area of health care and I can bring that to the role, based on my previous experience with hospitals.*'

Opening questions can take other forms, such as:

'*Why should we hire you?*'

'*Why did you apply?*'

'*Why should we choose you over another candidate?*'

The truth is, they are all the same question asked in different ways. The interviewer is trying to get a sense of your understanding of the role, your key skills and your enthusiasm.

Once the first few opening questions are asked, usually the interviewer will then look at your specific skills in detail.

Skills-based questions

The purpose of a job interview is to examine if a candidate is the right fit for the job. A CV will give a certain amount of information about a person's career but what it can't do is show the reality of someone's abilities, insights and attitudes.

For example, your CV might say you are a manager who leads a team of five people, but that doesn't mean you are necessarily a good manager with clear management strategies and leadership skills.

Equally, your CV may show you have worked as part of a team but you could have been a team member who contributed nothing and who refused to work with your colleagues to reach the end goal.

With that in mind, the main purpose of an interview is to get behind your CV and really understand the skills you could bring to the new role. To do this, interviewers will ask you to go into detail about your experience by providing an example of your skills. If you say you are a good team player you must prove that with an example. If you say you work on your own initiative you must prove that with an example.

There is a very simple step-by-step process you can use to answer these skills-based questions.

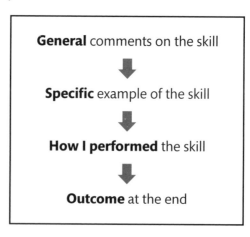

General comments on the skill

⬇

Specific example of the skill

⬇

How I performed the skill

⬇

Outcome at the end

When you are asked any sort of skills-based question in an interview, you need to go through these four stages in your answer. Let me show you how this works.

Going back to our project-manager role, imagine the question was: 'You have said you are very good with budgeting. Can you tell us a bit more about that?'

1. **General comments on the skill:** 'I believe having a clear budget and sticking to it is vital to the success of a project. I have dealt with lots of different-sized budgets but the most significant was for a hospital redesign I worked on for the health service.'

2. **Specific example of the skill:** 'As the project leader I had a budget of two million for the full redesign and I was in charge of managing it, paying all suppliers and ensuring we got the best value and service for our money.'

3. **How I performed the skill:**
   - 'I decided to get three quotes for every supplier, to ensure we had the best price.'
   - 'I set specific financial milestones to ensure we didn't go over budget.'
   - 'I created a detailed spreadsheet I could check-in with, daily and weekly, to ensure we were on track.'
   - 'I assigned a junior team member the task of checking the budget-spend and reporting anything out of the ordinary on a weekly basis.'

4. **Outcome:** 'The project came in on-time and on-budget, which I was very proud of, and I believe I can bring these skills to this role.'

These four steps can be applied to any skills-based question in an interview.

Closing questions

Once all the skills-based questions have been addressed, the interview will naturally begin to come to a close. At this stage there are a few other questions that may come up. They are:

'WHAT ARE YOUR STRENGTHS AND WEAKNESSES?'

This is a classic interview question that you need to be prepared to answer. Once again, please remember this is *'in relation to this role'* – don't start naming strengths or weaknesses that are not relevant.

Your strengths are the key skills you have that match the job description and your weaknesses are the areas you feel you still need to develop in relation to this role.

When you are asked about your weaknesses, do not answer with 'I work too hard' or 'I am a perfectionist'. This is avoiding the question, showing you have no insight into yourself and also making the interviewer worry you have something to hide.

If we go back to our project-manager example, the answer might look something like this:

'My strengths are my people skills and ability to deliver projects on-time and on-budget. My weakness in relation to this role will be getting up to speed with the computer system you use, as I have not used it in the past. However, I am a fast learner and willing to do whatever it takes to become competent in it as quickly as possible.'

What you want to do is identify a real weakness and then make sure you tell them you have a plan to address it, so it won't interfere with your ability to carry out the role.

'WHAT SALARY ARE YOU EXPECTING?'

It is suggested that you should not address salary until a job offer has been made. However, this question can and does come up in first interviews so you need to be prepared to answer it.

The most important thing with this question is to figure out the answer before you go for the interview, so you are not surprised or say something you will regret.

My only advice here is to decide your value and be honest. What is the lowest you will go? What do you want to be paid? Is that reasonable in this market for that role? Do some research to help you.

You are the person who has to live with the salary, so decide what you want and need and make sure it is reasonable, based on the current market, the role and your experience. Then just tell the truth when they ask the question.

'JAFFA CAKE – CAKE OR BISCUIT?'

A survey by recruitment agency Office Angels revealed that 90 per cent of employers pose what is called a 'killer question' at interviews:

'Who would you invite to a dinner party?'

'Tell us a joke.'

'Jaffa Cake – cake or biscuit?'

These are just some of the random or 'killer' questions that are being asked at interviews today.

They are intimidating questions, asked in a stressful environment, which are designed to see how you cope with pressure and think on your feet.

There is no way of knowing if you will be asked a killer question, or what the question might be. Here is a list of some of the most common killer questions asked at interviews to get you thinking (for more like these, visit www.linkedin.com/today/post/article/20130123154152-201849-32-killer-interview-questions):

1. What's the biggest mistake you made in your life and what did you learn from it?

2. What superhero would you be and why?

3. What is one misconception people have about you?

4. If you were a kitchen appliance what would you be?

5. Who at your former place of work gave you the most energy and why?

6. What do you think will be the biggest challenges you and I will face in your first three months on the job?

7. If you could wave a magic wand, what ill in the world would you solve and why?

8. You are on your deathbed; what do you want to be remembered for?

9. What was your most and least satisfying job and why?

10. When was the last time you lost your temper? What was the situation and why do you think this affects you so?

11. What motivates you and what doesn't?

12. Tell me in no more than two words what you think we do?

If you are asked any of these questions you need to pause, take a breath, ask them to repeat the question if you need them to and then answer as honestly as you can. They are looking not only at the answer but also at how you handle the stress of being asked this type of question.

'ANYTHING TO ADD?'

When the interview is closing, you will be asked if you have anything you would like to add.

This is a very important question and your last opportunity to say anything you need the interviewer to know. You do not want to leave the interview feeling you never got to talk about a particular example or skill because the question never came up.

Anything to add? . . . This is your last chance.

When this question comes, stop and ask yourself a few questions mentally:

- Did you answer every question as well as you could? If not, go back and have another go at it now.

- Did you get to talk about that really important project, skill or achievement? If not, do it now.

- Do they know how passionate you are about the role? Now is the time to tell them.

'DO YOU HAVE ANY QUESTIONS FOR US?'

You have reached the end of the interview. You have managed to say all the right things and then, just when you think you are in the clear, this final question comes.

This really can be a tough question to answer because the big fear is if you say nothing you will look disinterested and if you ask a question it might be the wrong question and you will fall at the last hurdle.

You should do your best to have two or three genuine (that being the important part) questions prepared about the role. For example:

- 'Do you have a full team in place for this project already?'

- 'What is the lead-in time for the project?'

- 'Will there be teams from your global office involved in the project?'

You want to steer clear of asking about holidays, time off and lunch breaks at this stage. Keep it very professional and specific to the role.

Do prepare some questions, as this is a great opportunity to get some insight into the role and the company and to show you are really interested.

What's in it for you?

Job interviews are a test of how you handle stress, as well as an assessment of your fit for the role.

You can be interviewed by your colleagues, complete strangers or, worse, people you know and don't respect. You can be asked anything and, no matter how prepared you are, a question you didn't expect can come up.

Today, companies such as Google, Facebook and LinkedIn expect you to sit up to six interviews for one role.

Communicating effectively at a job interview is essential for your career success. Job interviews are something you can do very well at if you prepare before you speak.

Chapter cheat sheet

The whole point of a job interview is to sell yourself:

Selling yourself in a job interview does not mean:
- you lie or exaggerate;
- you make big statements you can't back up;
- you are loud and arrogant.

GET OVER IT!

Selling yourself at a job interview is about:
- understanding the role and the skills needed;
- telling the interviewer that you have those skills;
- proving you have those skills by using real examples and evidence from your career.

How to ruin your chances:
- not preparing for the interview;
- not listening to the questions or answering the wrong question;
- providing irrelevant information;
- making negative comments about yourself, thus showing a lack of confidence;
- not taking opportunities to sell yourself;
- not showing enthusiasm or passion.

There are three parts of a job interview you need to prepare for:
- the opening questions;
- the skills-based questions;
- the closing questions.

These four steps can be applied to any skill-based question in an interview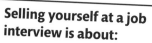

General comments on the skill

Specific example of the skill

How I performed the skill

Outcome at the end

The approach: The three steps in action

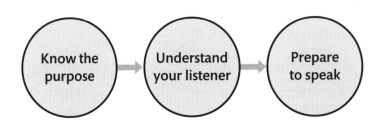

Know the purpose → Understand your listener → Prepare to speak

Ninety per cent of the success of your verbal communication is determined before you speak.

90%

In order to succeed at one-to-one conversations, giving feedback, job interviews, networking, facilitation and media, there are three steps you must take before you speak.

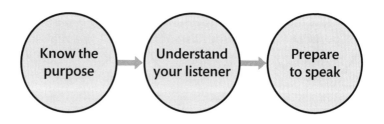

In each chapter so far, and in the final two chapters in Section 3, we are exploring the concepts around this approach.

What I would like to do now is turn these concepts into something concrete that you can use to succeed in your interactions.

This three-step approach I am offering must be done in sequence. You must have absolute clarity about the purpose of the communication first. Once you know or decide this then you must profile your audience and understand them. Finally, armed with your intention and listener-insight, you will prepare what to say and how to say it to ensure your goal is reached.

Over the next few pages I am going to give you some simple templates that can be used to help you prepare your communication for each of the business scenarios in this book.

STEP 1
Know the purpose

In order to prepare great verbal communication you need a communication goal. You also need to know how you are going to reach your goal.

For example:

What is the purpose of my communication in this job interview?
To get the job.

What information does the listener need in order to achieve this purpose?
I need to communicate to the interviewer that I understand the role, my strengths and my passion in order to get the job.

Is it possible to give all the information and reach the purpose in this one exchange?
This is the first interview so I know I will not get a job offer from it, but I want to do enough to get to a second interview.

Before you engage in any of the business scenarios explored in this book, the first step in preparing is to ask yourself these three questions:

1. What is the purpose of this communication/interaction?

2. How do I bring my listener to that end-goal?

3. Is it possible to get that outcome in this one exchange?

Is it possible in this one exchange?

Once you are clear on your purpose, you must ask yourself if it is possible to achieve it in just one exchange. Sometimes it takes many meetings and interactions to actually reach your purpose, and this first one is just a stepping-stone on the path to that point.

For example, your overall networking goal may be to get new business; however, you may have several meetings where the purpose is to build a relationship, understand the potential client's business or simply swap ideas.

Every single interaction is different and will have a different purpose. It is vital you are clear what the communication purpose is before you can prepare what to say.

I want you to like me

For many people, their communication purpose is to be liked, admired or recognised in some way. Very often this is their only goal when they speak.

Of course you want to be liked and thought highly of. I want this for you too. However, this can't be your only purpose as it is too self-serving. Remember, people engage and connect with you because there is something in it for them. The more you focus on your listener and on giving them something of value when you speak, the more they will think you are great.

The personal purpose for your communication is always one of being well-liked and respected, and that is OK.

For example: 'I want the interviewer to like me and think I am smart'.

However, you must make sure you have a *purposeful purpose* and not just a *personal purpose*. (Try saying that really fast!)

A purposeful purpose is:

'I will make sure the interviewer has all the information about me they need to make the decision to give me the job. While giving that information I will do my best to do it in a way that shows my passion, credibility and knowledge in the hope they like me and think I am smart.'

Below is a template to help you get clarity on the purpose of your communication and how it can be achieved.

This template can be applied to every business scenario in this book.

This is step one of your preparation.

Step 1: know the purpose template

What is the purpose of my communication/interaction today?

What information does the listener need in order to achieve that purpose?

Is it possible to give all the information and reach the purpose in this one exchange?

STEP 2
Understand the listener

If you don't mind, I would like at this point to tell you a little bit about me. My name is Emma Ledden and, according to the Myers-Briggs Type Indicator® assessment, I am an ESTJ (extraversion, sensing, thinking, judgement). My social style is a 'driver' and I am an 'activist' in my learning style. Based on these labels, I am an externally-focused and enthusiastic person. I don't like waiting, indirectness or indecisiveness. I am apparently principled, independent and intellectually creative.

On any given day I can be tired, stressed, interested or inspired. If you meet me just before lunchtime, I am probably hungry and it's best not to speak to me. I am neither inviting nor charming while in need of food. One day I may be standing in front of you smiling, hiding a broken heart. On another day, on another week, I might be in such a good place in my life I forget pain exists, for me or for you.

And on a bad day, if you disregard me in any way, even by accident, the most insecure and vulnerable part of me is triggered and you will no longer be dealing with a grown adult, instead you will have a seven-year-old in front of you, emotionally at least.

Why am I telling you all this? Because we are all the same. I am you and you are me.

We are all human, we are all emotional and we are interacting and communicating with each other every day.

The people you are talking to in your everyday exchanges are human beings, and you need to remember and prepare for this before you speak.

You need to consider what your listener knows, thinks and feels about your information before you speak. You need to prepare for your listener's reactions, questions and feedback to your communication. You need to do all this before you speak.

In the future, before you speak you must understand your listener by clarifying:

- What does my listener think, know and feel before I talk?

- What do I want them to think, know and feel after I talk?

Talking to different people with different needs

Talking to one person with one set of needs and emotions is a challenge, so talking to a group with possibly many different needs can feel overwhelming.

When faced with an audience, rather than just one person, the default can be to give an outpouring of general information not tailored at anyone in the hope of it satisfying everyone. This rarely works and leaves both the speaker and listeners unfulfilled.

It is hard to cater to a mixed group of listeners, and although they can't all be talked to at once, their needs can be addressed one by one during your communication in a way that gives them something of value.

If you have a mixed group of listeners you must understand what the needs are within the group and you must decide if you are going to address all of these needs as part of the purpose of the communication. The choice is yours, based on what you want to achieve and your communication purpose.

Timing is everything

They say in life timing is everything. I am sure you have had moments in your life, both successful and disastrous, that have had some element of timing attached to them.

An important part of understanding your listener is asking the question of yourself – is this the right time to have this conversation or exchange?

I don't mean for the timing element to be a tool for procrastination or refusal to have a conversation that needs to happen. But, before you speak just consider: is this the right moment of the day, day of the week or week of the month to speak? Are you ready, emotionally and mentally, to speak and are they ready to listen (within reason)?

In business you must have the conversation, but just make sure you pick the best possible time to have it.

Below is a simple template to help you understand your listener.

This template can be applied to every business scenario in this book.

This is step two of your preparation.

Step 2: understand the listener template

Who is my listener?

Before I speak, what does my listener know, think and feel about my information?

Know:
Think:
Feel:

After I speak, what do I want my listener to know, think and feel?

Know:
Think:
Feel:

STEP 3
Prepare to speak

This book explores six business scenarios.

On the pages that follow are templates to help you prepare what to say in each individual scenario.

You must complete step one and step two, as explained, and then, depending on the interaction, choose the relevant template and fill it out in full before you speak.

This is step three in your preparation.

Step 3: prepare to speak – one-to-one communication template

What is the opening hook for this communication that tells my listener why they should listen?

| |
| |

What are my three key points or areas I wish to explain and talk about in this interaction?

One	Two	Three

What is my concluding, take-away point or action I wish to leave the listener with?

| |
| |

Step 3: prepare to speak – giving feedback template

Event: What specific examples of the behaviour do I have?	Effect: What is the impact of this behaviour on the team, management or client/customer?	Change or continue: What behaviour needs to change or be continued?

Step 3: prepare to speak – networking template

Name of the event:
The three people I want to speak to:
1.
2.
3.
Possible conversation topics:
1.
2.
3.
4.
5.
How will I follow up?

Step 3: prepare to speak – job interview template

The job I am going for:

Why am I the right person for this job?

What are the key skills required for this role?

What are my specific examples for each skill?

What is my weakness in relation to this role?

Any questions for them?

Step 3: prepare to speak – facilitation template

H - Hook and context
O - Outline of what you will cover
L - Link to real life and long-term benefit
A - Any other business - breaks and housekeeping

H	
O	
L	
A	

Step 3: prepare to speak – media interview template

Name of show:		
What are my key messages for the audience of the show?	What are my stories, examples, interesting facts or case studies that will make my messages understandable for the audience?	What kind of questions will I be asked, both positive and negative?

Section 3

Communicating to groups

Communicating
to facilitate

STEP 1
Know the purpose

Facilitation is leading or guiding a group so they achieve a common goal.

You can facilitate workshops, training courses and meetings, both internally within your company and externally with a client or public group.

Great facilitating is like being a party host. You begin plagued with the usual questions of will anyone turn up, will they have fun and will they behave themselves? (There is always one.) Then there is all the planning and preparation. You are in charge of the entire experience and you need to have everything ready when people arrive.

Finally, on the day itself, you work very hard to make sure everyone is having the best possible time, catering to everyone's needs until they all leave and you collapse from exhaustion probably feeling like you coulda/shoulda/woulda done more.

The difference between presenting and facilitating

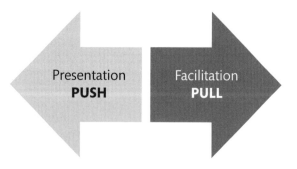

The most important thing to say at this stage is that facilitation is not presentation, and presenting is not facilitating.

Presenters focus on giving one-way information. This is a perfect dynamic to deliver some key messages but it will not lead to any behaviour change, new skills development or sharing of experiences.

If the goal is to give the listener or the group a new skill, share experiences or change behaviour in the long term, you can't just stand at the top of a room lecturing to a group. You must create an experience that allows for two-way communication.

In order to create this experience, you must facilitate, not present.

The skill of a facilitator involves:

- conveying information in a way that allows the participants to explore the topic and come to their own conclusions;

- using questioning and active listening;

- managing group activities and discussions;

- responding to the listeners' behaviours and the group dynamic.

A facilitator must get information across to gain engagement and stimulate discussion, but then they must manage the discussion, listen and pull out the key learnings for the group.

The truth is, facilitators need to do a mix of presenting and facilitating – a mix of pushing and pulling.

The fact of facilitation

There is a very famous saying from Benjamin Franklin:

> 'Tell me and I forget, teach me and I may remember, involve me and I learn.'
>
> **BENJAMIN FRANKLIN**

Turns out that he was right.

How we learn

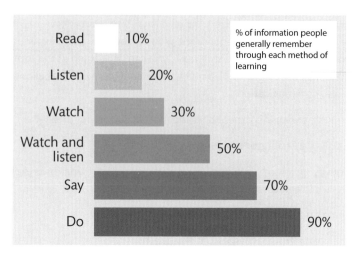

Source: Figure derived from Dale, E. (1946) *Audio-visual methods in teaching*, New York: The Dryden Press.

Facilitation is the skill of telling, showing and allowing the listener to experience. This guarantees the best possible result and retention. Facilitating helps people to learn on their own, rather than telling them what to do.

Facilitators use questioning and listening skills to lead a group and, most importantly, a facilitator gives the group time and space to understand, learn and contribute.

THE SKILL-SET OF A GREAT FACILITATOR

- Communication skills
- Questioning and listening skills (as discussed in Chapter 1)
- Patience
- Confidence
- Approachability
- Understanding and empathy
- Good knowledge of the topic (does not have to be an expert)

The facilitator is 100 per cent responsible for the experience created for a group, so they must:

- prepare their own materials and work out a training timetable;

- ensure the room is suitable, and properly laid out for a group of people;

- ensure all equipment is in working order before participants arrive;

- be present before participants arrive and ready to welcome them;

- greet each individual, learning their names and remembering them;

- introduce people if they don't already know one another;

- create a friendly and easy atmosphere;

- start and finish the session on time;

- be fully prepared, and deliver an engaging and interesting session.

STEP 2
Know your listener

The fundamental you need to always remember with facilitation in business is that you are dealing with an adult audience. Adults learn and contribute in a unique way that is different to how we learnt in school.

How adults learn

Pedagogy vs andragogy

Pedagogy: derived from the Greek words 'ped', meaning 'child' and 'agogus', meaning 'leader of'. Therefore, pedagogy literally means the science of leading (teaching) children.

Andragogy: described as 'the art and science of helping adults learn' and could be seen as the opposite of the pedagogical approach.

As a facilitator you will be applying an andragogical approach, so you need to bear in mind the following.

What's in it for me?

Remember this guy?

W.I.F.M?

Adults need to know *why* they need to learn. Adults have a keen desire to establish 'What's in it for me?' before they invest in the process.

You need to emphasise the importance of the training event or workshop in terms of improving your participants' jobs and lives.

The need to build on their experience

Adults have developed experience over many years, which needs to be tapped into using appropriate methods. These methods include:

- group discussion;
- role-plays;
- case studies;
- problem-solving activities.

I will go into these in more detail later in the chapter, but the most important thing to know is that a group of adults will learn far more from each other than they will from listening solely to a facilitator. If you are to successfully implement the androgogical model, you need to know your listeners and design a facilitation session that meets their needs.

Learning to ride a bike

Do you remember learning to ride your first bike?

Can you remember if you:

- jumped straight on the bike and just had a go;

- thought about riding the bike a while before getting on;

- needed to understand the mechanics of the bike and how it operated before you could ride it;

- looked for some practical tips from a bike-riding expert (i.e. your mum or dad) before you jumped on.

Whether it is learning to ride a bike or participating in any other learning, we all have different learning styles. There are four learning styles, as found by Peter Honey and Alan Mumford (see www.peterhoney.com):

- **Activist**: if you are an activist you like fast-paced sessions that involve doing and experiencing things. You are eager to jump feet first into any activity, with little or no instruction. You don't like sitting around, working alone or too much theory.

- **Reflector**: if you are a reflector you need time – time to look, time to absorb, time to think, time to answer and time to write. You cannot be rushed and you don't like going first.

- **Theorist**: this is the one learning style that needs the detail and the background. You want to know how it all fits and then you want to analyse and check it to be sure. You like ideas and concepts. You do not like anything silly or unclear.

- **Pragmatist**: this learning style needs the session to be practical, related to the real world and have concrete applications. You love tools, techniques and processes you can implement afterwards. You do not like anything with no relevance or that is intangible.

When you are facilitating a group it could be made up of:

- all activists (my idea of heaven);

- all theorists (my idea of hell);

- a mix of all four styles (most likely).

And... don't forget you also have a learning style as a facilitator, and your default will be to design and run the workshop or meeting the way you prefer.

For example, I am an activist. Therefore I am a reflector's and theorist's worst nightmare. My default is to give zero instruction and expect instant reactions. I even get a bit huffy when they are thinking (reflecting).

Therefore, I must make sure, when I am designing and running a workshop, that I give proper instructions, good written hand-outs and time and space for thought.

STEP 3
Prepare to speak

There are three factors of great facilitation:

1. The real start and the right start;

2. Information to interaction;

3. Managing the group.

The real start

The role of a facilitator begins before the start of the workshop or meeting. You must design the session in full. To design a facilitation session, start by answering these questions:

- By the end of the facilitation, what do you want everyone to leave with? What information do you need from them by the end of the day? Always start with the end in mind.

- Who is in your group? Are they coming to you willingly or is it mandatory? Do they know why they are attending and what the purpose of the day is?

- What is the structure of the session? How many key areas are you going to cover? Is there enough time to cover all you want?

- Do you want people to work in small groups or do you want open discussion in one whole group? Do you want a mix of both?

- When are you taking breaks/stopping for lunch?

- How are you capturing ideas? How many flipcharts and markers do you need? Are you using technology?

- Do you need to send some pre-information? Would that help everyone come in the right frame of mind to the session (remember the theorists)?

The right start

The opening of your facilitation on the day itself is the most important part. You must start on time. The group must know things will run on time and on target. You set the standard for this.

If a number of participants have not yet turned up, you may delay the start time by five minutes, but only by five minutes, and only with the prior agreement of those who have arrived on time.

Don't say hello, say HOLA

At the beginning of your workshop or meeting, your participants are sitting there with all sorts of thoughts running through their minds – for example:

- Who is this person? (If they don't know you.)

- What time will this finish?

- What is this going to be about?

- Will it be interesting?

- Why am I here?

As we just explored in the previous section, each individual in the group is simply thinking WIIFM – what's in it for me?

And you need to make sure you begin your meeting or workshop with a clear and structured answer to this question.

How? By saying HOLA.

> **H** – Hook and context
> **O** – Outline of what you will cover
> **L** – Link to real life and long-term benefit
> **A** – Any other business – breaks and housekeeping

Let me give you an example of how to apply this in real life. Imagine I am running a one-day workshop on facilitation skills, with six managers who, in turn, will be designing and running workshops of their own over the next 12 months:

H

'Hi, my name is Emma Ledden and you are very welcome to this course called "Facilitating With Impact". You are all going to be designing and running workshops over the next 12 months; I want to help you do that as confidently and competently as possible.'

O

'The main areas I will cover today are:
- *creating engaging communication, visuals and hand-outs;*
- *questioning and listening;*
- *dealing with groups.'*

L

'These skills will help you become a better facilitator and will also help you in client meetings, team projects and presentations in the future.

The session is very practical and tailored around you. I will record you facilitating on a camera and play you back to yourself so you can get awareness of your personal facilitation and presentation style. I will also give you detailed feedback.'

A

'We will take two coffee breaks and a lunch break, and finish at 5pm. All I ask is for everyone to please turn your phone and laptop off before we begin.'

Should I set ground rules?

One strategy for ensuring your group works together is to begin the day with a list of ground rules about how the group must behave during the meeting or workshop.

You can look at setting ground rules around these areas at the beginning of your course:

- switching off mobile phones;

- punctuality;

- confidentiality;

- listening to each other;

- asking questions;

- being open to new ideas;

- having fun;

- treating each other with respect;

- guidelines for giving and receiving feedback.

I have been a trainer for 10 years and I have never set formal ground rules or asked any group I work with to set them. I do ask for phones and laptops to be turned off, but that is as far as I go. I feel ground rules are too much like school, and I trust that if my opening HOLA is good enough I will gain and keep attention.

In my experience, adult learners are well able to behave properly and they don't like being patronised, which I fear is what ground rules can do.

This is my opinion, based on my experience. You will have to make the decision whether or not to set ground rules for yourself and your group.

The ultimate combo – introductions and ice-breakers

Once you have said HOLA, the next step is to understand what your participants need from the session. You also need to have an ice-breaker to give the group a chance to get comfortable with each other.

The idea with an ice-breaker is to relieve some of the normal tension that exists in a room with a group of adult learners who may or may not know each other, and who are possibly feeling nervous about the day.

Ice-breakers are about breaking down barriers, creating a more pleasant learning environment and facilitating learning. A 'good atmosphere' is not accidental – it can and should be created by the facilitator.

A TOUR OF THE TABLE

If you have a group of fewer than eight people you can simply go around the group one by one, asking each person their name, their personal challenges in the area you are covering and their goal for the training.

Even though it may seem that way on the surface, this is not a simple question-and-answer session. This is a discussion with the purpose of bonding the group, finding common ground and relieving some tension. Take your time and allow a dynamic to develop as you question each person. Find common themes and link people together in their expectations of the day, their challenges or their goals.

A tour of the table is not your only option for an introduction and icebreaker. You can be more adventurous, depending on the age and size of the group. Here are a few other examples of introductions and icebreakers.

1. **Youngest to oldest:** this works really well for larger groups (over 12 people and under the age of 30). I ask everyone to stand in line, youngest to oldest, facing me. Then I get each person to tell the group their name, their goal for the session and one interesting thing about themselves.

2. **Interview each other and introduce:** with a smaller group (around 10–12 people), I put the participants into pairs and ask them to interview each other and then present back on the person they are talking to. The questions remain the same: their name, their goal for the day and one interesting thing about themselves.

3. **The M&M intro:** put a packet of chocolate M&Ms in a bowl and ask each person in the group to take one but not to eat it just yet. Put up a slide showing the M&M colours and a corresponding question, such as this:

- Red – best holiday you ever had
- Green – your childhood nickname
- Brown – favourite country you ever visited
- Yellow – your party piece.

Ask each person to tell the room their name, their goal for the training and the answer to the question that corresponds with their M&M colour. Then they get to eat it!

Information to interaction

The heart of facilitation lies in getting the group to do the work, rather than the facilitator doing the work.

There a number of ways to do this using the tools below:

- **Group discussions**: a way of exchanging thoughts and ideas for a set period of time in one large group or in smaller groups. Groups can talk generally about the topic, having a set outcome from the discussion as decided by the facilitator.

- **Role-plays**: role-plays have been part of learning experiences for a long time and are a way of practising or rehearsing a scenario that may happen in real life. For example, presentations or customer interactions can be practised and perfected in a workshop.

- **Case studies**: these are very useful in facilitations as they tend to replicate a real-life situation. Using case studies is a way to explore all the possible angles and outcomes of a situation in a safe environment.

- **Problem-solving activities**: having interactive activities, such as having to build a LEGO tower in groups to demonstrate teamwork or an exercise to organise a weekend away for 10 people with no money, can get groups to interact in a fun and meaningful way.

Let me give you a very simple example of how I would use group discussions to explore the use of visual aids in my 'Facilitating With Impact' course.

Starting with my HOLA

H – Now we are going to look at using visual aids during a facilitation workshop and establish what is best practice.

O – The goal is to examine all the possible visual aids you can use and the pros and cons of each type.

L – This session will help you identify the best visuals to use in different scenarios and also how to prepare them.

A – You will be working in groups of three and each group will get a chance to present back to the room on a type of visual aid.

I then ask them to get into groups of three and do this series of exercises:

- Ask them to list all the possible visual aids you can use in a facilitation.

- Assign a visual aid to each group, i.e. one group takes PowerPoint, one takes a flipchart and one takes a hand-out.

- Ask them to come up with their version of best practice, including pros and cons, for their visual aid – based on their experience.

- Ask them to present back to the room as a group on their visual aid's best practice rules.

Once this is completed, as the facilitator, I can now fill in any gaps that may have been left out.

The goal of facilitation is to make the group do the work, as opposed to just presenting the information at them.

Managing the group

I have been facilitating and training groups for 10 years now. The part I find the most challenging is managing the group dynamic.

Great facilitation looks like this:

A great facilitator is like a great shepherd. They allow the participants (the sheep) to move from one area to another while keeping everyone safe and keeping the flock intact.

Great facilitation has a clear agenda, starts on time, sticks to time and moves the group to an end-goal, while allowing space to share and debate.

Bad facilitation looks like this:

Bad facilitation has the participants (the sheep) running all over the place, baaing like crazy and behaving out of control.

Keeping your participants safe and getting them to the end-goal intact is a challenge for any facilitator.

At any time, a participant can behave in a negative way, which may have a destructive impact on the group and on the learning. These are some of the behaviours you will come across and will need to manage:

- **Dominating the group:** taking up a great deal of time with comments and questions that may or may not be relevant.

- **Acting superior:** trying to appear more skilled and knowledgeable than the others in the group or the facilitator.

- **Arriving late after breaks:** turning up late in the morning and after breaks, giving the impression of a lack of commitment to the session.

- **On their phones:** continually distracted by and responding to messages under the table or in plain sight.

- **Side conversations:** two or more participants who are continually having whispered conversations.

- **Complaining:** continually finding fault with the programme and the facilitator.

- **Being unprepared:** not having pre-work completed.

- **Not engaging:** not participating in activities.

- **Clowning:** joking at inappropriate times, distracting others.

There are several reasons why negative behaviours occur. For example, the participant:

- does not understand the relevance of the programme;

- is afraid of failing or being exposed on the programme;

- has outside pressures and deadlines;

- likes to debate and question data before they accept it as fact;

- enjoys being the centre of attention;

- is not comfortable doing an activity such as role-play in front of the group.

No matter the reason, when you are faced with a problem behaviour that will impact negatively on your group, you must act to manage that behaviour as best you can.

WHEN FACED WITH A DISRUPTIVE PARTICIPANT YOU MUST:

1. **Manage your own emotions:** negative behaviour shows disrespect, which can trigger you emotionally. As a facilitator you may feel defensive or angry.

2. **Manage the group:** make sure you are not monopolised by this one person, as you're responsible for the whole group.

3. **Manage the person:** you will need to deal directly with the person and their negative behaviour.

In order to do these three things, you need to not take the behaviour personally and you need to intervene using the 'Levels of influence'.

The 'Levels of influence' is a simple concept that may help you in this area.

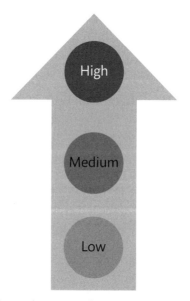

The 'Levels of influence' suggests that, as a general rule, if you have a difficult participant you start by addressing their behaviour in the least impactful way first.

Low-level influence

For example, if you have two people in your group having a side conversation, the following may be the first ways you might try to intervene and solve it:

- give direct eye contact to the pair and hold it for longer than usual;

- pause and wait until you have everyone's attention;

- move closer to the people concerned.

Medium-level influence

If your problem persists, it may be necessary to move up a level. For example:

- Set up a group activity (in pairs, or small groups) that will change the dynamic in the room and separate the pair so they are no longer sitting together.

- Stop the workshop and have a discussion with the group about the original ground rules, if you set them.

- Have a conversation with the pair over the break and ask them why they are not engaged in the programme.

High-level influence

At the top end of the 'Levels of influence' are the more drastic actions you can take – even asking someone to leave the group. You should never have to do this except in a very extreme case as it would represent a failure on the part of the facilitator. You should expect to be able to manage challenging situations in a positive way without making ultimatums or causing things to escalate.

When I began working as a facilitator I was told you will always 'lose control of one group in your career'. I have yet to completely lose a group but I have come close a few times.

Each facilitator has their own style, and groups respond differently to different people and situations. There is no 'one size fits all' in terms of group dynamics. Over time you will develop your own style and ways to manage your groups as a facilitator.

What's in it for you?

Facilitation is a powerful skill to master in business as it allows you to interact with others in a very engaging and authentic way. It challenges you to be listener-focused, which is at the heart of great communication.

The ability to listen well and ask questions, all the while genuinely caring about the experience you are creating, will allow you to run great meetings, have better relationships and be a great leader to your team.

Chapter cheat sheet

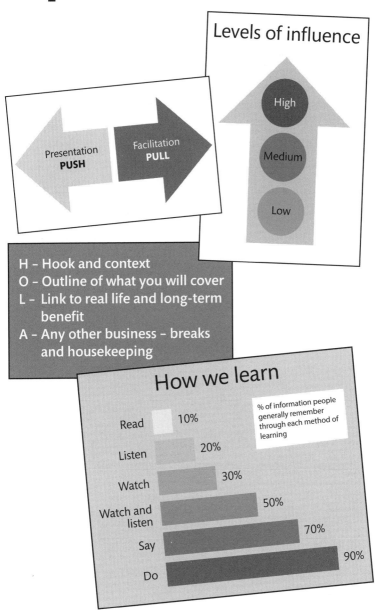

Levels of influence

High

Medium

Low

Presentation
PUSH

Facilitation
PULL

H – Hook and context
O – Outline of what you will cover
L – Link to real life and long-term
    benefit
A – Any other business – breaks
    and housekeeping

How we learn

% of information people generally remember through each method of learning

Read — 10%

Listen — 20%

Watch — 30%

Watch and listen — 50%

Say — 70%

Do — 90%

Communicating
on media

STEP 1
Know the purpose

More and more business people are being asked to contribute to the media today. A media contributor is someone who is invited to be part of a discussion and contribute their views on a topic.

Alternatively, the media may request an interview with you as part of a personal profile segment on you or your business.

The purpose of this chapter is not to tell you how to get onto media or build a PR strategy. I am afraid that is a whole other book, and you may need to pay for professional support if this is your goal.

This chapter is designed to help you perform on traditional broadcast media, if such an opportunity arises.

I am going to talk specifically about radio and television interviews. However, many of the concepts and ideas explored in this chapter apply to print-media interviews and video interviews for social media.

Should I always say 'Yes' to a media interview?

My answer is '**No**'... I will give you a minute to think about that.

The right interview on the right show can be very powerful but the wrong interview on the wrong show could do your personal brand considerable damage.

Take, for example, the difference between tabloid media and business media.

Tabloid media will always take a personal angle on a story so, if you engage in tabloid media, you must be prepared to talk about your personal life. Business media, on the other hand, will not normally ask whom you are dating or how you spend your free time.

But 'all publicity is good publicity' – right?

No it's not. All publicity will give you profile (a level of fame), but what will you be famous for?

Jordan (aka Katie Price) is a famous woman in the media and so is Angela Merkel – but for *very different reasons*.

Both have public profiles and both appear and are involved in the media regularly, but in a very different way.

If Angela Merkel decided to do a bikini shoot would she get publicity? Yes she would. Would it be the right publicity for her personal brand? I don't think so.

It's not easy to get an opportunity to speak on radio and television, so your instinct may be to say 'Yes' straight away; but before you say 'Yes' you must be sure the interview will add value to your brand.

You can say 'No' to the media (in the nicest possible way of course) if it is not right for you.

The media team

Generally, a TV or radio show will have the following team members:

- presenter;
- producer;
- researcher;
- runner.

There can and will be other people on the team, but these are the people you need to be aware of most:

- **Presenter**: the presenter is the person in front of the microphone or camera. They are the face or the voice of the show. They are the person who will be interviewing you on air.

- **Producer**: a producer is in charge of actually making the show. They (and there can be a team of producers on a show) decide what content, stories and interviews are happening on the show. The producer fundamentally decides how the show will run and what exactly will happen. Some presenters act as producers as well, but not all.

- **Researcher**: once the producer decides how the show will run, the researcher gets all the background information for the presenter. They source any clips, write questions and contact contributors and guests for the show.

- **Runner**: a runner makes endless cups of tea, looks after the guests when they come into studio and generally does anything and everything that needs to be done to support the producer, presenter and researcher.

If you are asked to contribute to a radio/TV show you will be contacted by either a producer or a researcher.

How and where the interview can happen

Interviews can happen in many different ways:

- **Pre-recorded interviews**: these interviews are recorded in advance either in the studio, your office or another location.

- **Live over the phone**: your interview will happen live over the phone rather than in the studio.

- **Live in a radio studio**: you will be asked to travel to the radio show and do the interview there, individually or as part of a panel.

- **Live in a TV studio**: you will be asked to travel to the TV studio to appear on the show.

Ask questions – as many as you like

I have worked with many producers and researchers and I can tell you without hesitation that it is OK to ask as many questions as you want and need to feel comfortable when going on media. They want you to feel comfortable because they want you to do your best.

Later in this chapter I will give you some tips on how to behave before, during and after a media interview. However, every team is different and every studio is different so I can't possibly address every situation that may arise in the media for you here.

If in doubt, or if you are just curious, ask.

STEP 2
Understand your listener

The business of media

I began my career in TV. Television is the business of making programmes that people will watch.

Television does not exist without an audience. A TV shows needs people to watch it, so it can get advertising. No audience means no advertising, which means no money.

When a TV show is being planned, perhaps the most important question the producers consider is 'Who is going to watch this?'.

The producers don't make any money or get their message across unless they know their audience. Once they know this they can begin to shape their TV show to appeal to this group.

The most important element of any TV show is an understanding of the target audience. This allows the producers to craft a show that will appeal directly to their audience and what is important to them.

The media knows there is no such thing as the 'general public'. A single, 21-year-old guy will be interested in very different things to a married, 55-year-old woman with three children.

The media ensures, no matter what is talked about, that it is tailored to the appropriate audience. Each TV and radio show has a target audience. Think for a second about your favourite TV show, the websites you visit, the magazines you read – I bet they are aimed at you and your peers.

If you are going on media you need to understand that your goal is to talk to the show's audience, watching or listening at home.

How do you know who is listening?

It is not all that difficult to examine whom the audience might be for any TV or radio show.

Some questions to ask are: what time of day is the show on; what kind of advertising is done on the show; and what angles do they take on current news stories?

Are people listening in their cars on their way to work, or are they stay-at-home parents or pensioners?

You can also ask the researcher or producer directly whom the show is aimed at and they will be happy to tell you.

The 'real' audience

One of the most important lessons I learnt early on in my career is that the presenter is just a telephone through which to talk to the audience.

The presenter of the show is not the audience but the presenter asks the question on behalf of the people at home. You do want to have a rapport with the presenter, but the person at home is whom you want to communicate with and persuade.

STEP 3
Prepare to speak

Please don't go on any sort of media if you:

- are shy;

- don't want to talk;

- don't want to talk about your topic;

- don't want to answer certain questions;

- are afraid the interviewer will bring a certain topic up and you don't want to talk about it (they will bring it up, even if they say they won't);

- don't want to debate every possible angle around your topic;

- are not prepared for the expected, the unexpected and absolutely everything in between.

A great media interview is like a great tennis match. It consists of two people, dressed in cute outfits, playing offence and defence, using both their forehand and backhand to hit a ball (answer questions) strategically, which is flying at them at a tremendous speed. Each player must have great stamina and give all of themselves for the entire duration of the match.

The media wants a great tennis match. They want energy and excitement. They want what's new this moment – what is yesterday is old. They want what's interesting. They want extremes, not normality.

You must be willing and able to do this if you are going on media. You must be able to talk about interesting things and not just go on and advertise yourself. No interviewer or presenter will let you do this.

If you want to go on media and talk about how great you are, you need to buy some advertising. Otherwise you have to bring something of interest and value to the table.

You may have noticed in this book that I do not talk about presentation skills. There is a reason for this: in September 2013 I published my first book, called *The Presentation Book*, where I covered this topic in great detail.

My interview

As part of the publicity for this book, I did a radio interview, which I feel is a very typical example of a media interview.

I would like to take you through each part of this media interaction, in the hope of showing you how the media works and what you can learn from my interview.

'I was contacted by the researcher of a radio show by email and asked would I go on an afternoon radio show for 30 minutes to talk about topics of the day, including a little interview on my book. They asked me what day I could do within the next week. They told me to come to the studio 30 minutes early, with five topical news stories to talk about. I had to have the news stories emailed to the researcher by 11am on the day of the interview and she would call me at 11.30 to talk through my stories.'

LEARNING FOR YOU

There are really only two ways to get on media: you contact them via press release, or they contact you having seen or heard about you, possibly from another source of media. In this case they heard I had written a book and they contacted me by email to invite me for the interview.

When the media contacts you the interview will usually happen within a short time-frame – it could be that day for some stories or maybe within the week if it is a more general interview topic. In this case they contacted me on a Wednesday and I agreed to do the interview the following Monday at 1pm in their studio.

They asked me to prepare some topics to talk about and we agreed to talk the morning of the interview. I spent the next few days preparing my stories and we talked as planned at 11.30am on the morning of the interview.

'I arrived at the studio 30 minutes before I was due to be interviewed. I went to reception, was greeted by the researcher and she asked me to sit in a waiting area. I sat reading the paper. Five minutes before the interview, I was brought into the studio.'

LEARNING FOR YOU

I travelled to the studio myself. I made my way to the reception area. I was seated and waited in the general area till I was called. You need to be there early, around 30 minutes before, but normally you will not be brought into the studio until the very last minute. Do not expect to be minded or given any special treatment.

If you do have questions, ask them before you get to the studio if possible. When you are at the studio the team will be very busy working on the show and they will not be able to give you very much time or attention. There are certain shows (mainly on TV) that have waiting areas called green rooms with food, drink and lots of attention, but this does not happen on radio in my experience.

'When it was time to go into the studio I was greeted by the interviewer, who was distracted trying to tee up the show and listen to the producer through his headphones. I said 'Hello' and handed him a copy of my book. He made a face and put the book down.'

LEARNING FOR YOU

Every interviewer is different. Every interviewer has a different style. Some will come out of the studio and greet you (if they have time), others will just expect you to be grateful to be there and to get on with it. On that day I was greeted with the latter.

He certainly wasn't thrilled to see me and if I thought

giving him a copy of my book was going to get him on side, I thought wrong.

He was very busy getting ready for the show so I sat down, put my headphones on (you need to do this) and waited for the show to begin and the first question to come.

'He began the interview with general questions about presentations. At first it seemed to be going well, but then, suddenly, he began asking questions in relation to selling and lying in a sales pitch. He accused me of teaching people to lie and that presenting to sell was about spin. It was the worst possible angle he could have chosen, from my point of view.'

LEARNING FOR YOU

When you are interviewed by a radio or television presenter you must be aware that their knowledge of you and your topic may be limited to:

1. a press release;
2. a Google search or some other research handed to them by the researcher;
3. their own opinions about you and the topic you are discussing.

From this starting point they can go wherever they want with the interview.

In this case the interview started off well until suddenly he started asking me about selling and lying in presentations. What became crystal clear very quickly was that he hadn't actually read the book and he had taken the name of my business, 'Presenting To Sell', put two and two together and got five.

The questions he asked were not relevant to my work or the book. He started talking about teaching people spin and lying. He brought the interview down this ▶

path and I had to follow him and then try and bring it back.

Every interviewer approaches an interview with three things in mind:

- What's new?
- What's different?
- Why should we care?

A presenter will normally have some sort of format for their questioning:

- The first question will (in one form or another) be what's the story here?
- The last question will (in one form or another) be where do you go from here?
- In between, the presenter will deal with extremes:
  - What's the best?
  - What's the worst?
  - Why is this relevant, important, interesting?

'I did my best to answer his questions and manage my own emotion until he changed his line of questioning again a few minutes later.'

LEARNING FOR YOU

The first decision I had to make was whether I pointed out the fact that he clearly hadn't read the book. This was 100 per cent what I wanted to do, but rule number one of media interviews is do not ever make the presenter look bad. You do not want to expose or annoy them.

Next I had to really manage my own emotion. I was getting very rattled and angry with him for going down this route and I had to remind myself it was my job to answer the questions and not respond to the tone or emotion. I was shaking from the adrenaline in my body but I did my best to take deep breaths and not take it personally.

I had no choice but to address his questions as best I could by using examples and stories from my own experience and the book. After a few minutes of head-on questioning he backed off and went back to more straight-line questions.

'The slot lasted 30 minutes, although I did not talk for all that time. Not once was I asked about the five news stories I had prepared.'

LEARNING FOR YOU

The researcher can't speak for the presenter. The researcher may tell you that the presenter will or will not do something or say something but you can't take it as gospel or always believe it, because they simply can't speak for the person in the chair.

I was told I would talk about my five news stories and then maybe just a few minutes on the book. That was not what happened. I was not asked about my news stories once. The entire time was taken up with the book, which was fantastic, albeit unexpected.

'The interview finished, I said 'Thank you' and left. I went back to my office and I listened back to the show.'

LEARNING FOR YOU

I left the radio studio feeling very shaky. I was very uncertain as to how it had gone. I knew there was a moment I could have lost it. Did I? Did the three-second pause when he asked me whether I was teaching people to lie seem as long in real life as it did in my head? Did I manage my emotion or did I sound out of control on air?

▶

I could not answer any of these questions yet and my feelings at that time would only betray me as my fight-or-flight response had been triggered. I went back to my office and listened back to the interview in full online.

Thankfully, the interview was not as bad as I'd felt it was. It was interesting and lively, and although his questions were very challenging and not what I hoped, they did make for very good radio. This is his job. He did it very well.

'Finally, I emailed the researcher and said 'Thank you'.'

LEARNING FOR YOU

Later that day I emailed the researcher to say 'Thank you' and she sent me a copy of the show via email for my records. The other reason to email afterwards is the hope of maintaining a relationship of some sort with the researcher for the future.

Preparing for your media interview

The first step to preparing for a media interview is to ask a few questions:

- Who is the audience for this show?

- What is the topic I am talking about?

- What is the angle I want to give/what angle might they go with?

- Why am I being asked to speak?

- Will anyone else be on the show with me talking about this topic?

- Is it live or pre-recorded?

- Is it a phone interview or in a studio?

- What do I need to prepare for the interview?

A media interview is exactly the same as a one-to-one conversation in that you are trying to move your listener from where they are to where you want them to be.

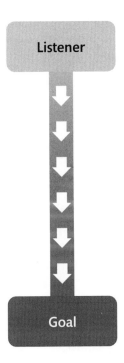

Once you are clear on the programme's audience, ask yourself what do they know about my topic and how do they feel about it before the interview?

Then, what do you want them to know and what do you want them to feel after your interview?

If you are unsure, try and speak to someone you know who might represent the target listener and ask them their thoughts or what they might find interesting.

You must prepare three things for a media interview:

1. The key points you want the listener to remember.

2. How to make those points interesting and understandable for the listener.

3. The kind of questions you are likely to be asked and how best to answer them.

Have a bottomless bag of great things to say

To succeed at a media interview, you must become Mary Poppins. The popular musical *Mary Poppins* is about a magical nanny who comes to look after two children. Mary Poppins has with her a bottomless carpet bag and, whatever situation arises, Mary is able to pull something from that bag to match the circumstances. She pulls out everything, from medicine to magical umbrellas.

It is impossible to know what questions you will be asked during a media interview. You can ask the interviewer or producer in advance to send you a list of questions. However, I will be very surprised (a) if they send you a list and (b) if they send you a list and stick to the questions.

What you need to succeed on media is your very own magic bottomless carpet bag of great things to say, no matter what question you are asked.

With that in mind, you must be clear on your key messages and then you must prepare your bottomless bag of great things to say around those messages. These include:

- relevant personal stories and examples;
- interesting facts or new information;
- case studies.

When you are asked a question during a TV or radio interview, you must pull the relevant story/fact/case study out of your magic bottomless bag of great things to say and deliver it to the audience at home in a way they can relate to and understand.

Studio protocols

Earlier in the chapter I talked about different ways you can be interviewed – over the phone, on radio or on television. Once you are clear on what you want to say during the interview, there are some other studio and interview protocols you need to be aware of and manage.

Telephone interviews

- Put a sign on your door saying 'Do not enter' and make sure there will be no other calls coming through to you during the interview.

- A landline is much better than a mobile.

- Stand up – it will allow you to breathe properly and it will make you feel 'I am on'.

Radio and television interviews

- Arrive at the studio 30 minutes before your interview time, unless told otherwise.

- In a TV studio do not move things around. The studio and the chair you are sitting in will be lit a certain way. (This takes hours!) You don't want to mess with the lighting guys – trust me.

- Whenever you are in the vicinity of a television camera or microphone you are always 'on' (i.e. people can see and hear you). Don't say anything you don't want a lot of people to hear.

- In some situations you may be given a radio microphone (portable microphone); **be careful**... don't go the toilet with the microphone on and don't go off and make a private phone call, as the sound guys can hear everything. You don't want to mess with them either, by the way.

- Always have a glass of water with you.

- Do not have a click pen, rustling paper or anything noisy in a studio.

- Live media works to very strict timings. Be aware of these timings and don't take it personally if you get cut off by the interviewer. If you are doing a pre-recorded interview, timing is not as big an issue – however, you may want to give yourself a time deadline. Tell them you have only 20 minutes. The more you say, the more they can edit it to look however they want.

- 'Off the record': this is a term that means you say something to a interviewer but they won't broadcast it, or at least they won't attribute it to you if they do say it. I do not advise you to work 'off the record' unless you are sure you can trust the interviewer or presenter.

- In a radio studio, make sure you are not too close or too far away from the microphone; aim for the length of your middle finger as the perfect distance.

- Do not bring your mobile phone into a TV or radio studio.

- At the end of an interview, hold still till you are given the all-clear by the presenter or another member of the team.

- Do not look at the camera at any time when you are on television or are being interviewed – you are not the presenter.

- An interviewer is not your friend. Presenters can be very good at making you feel comfortable to the point where you forget where you are and you may say something you will regret.

- Going into a radio or TV studio is very exciting and a little daunting if it is your first time. It is important to try and be as normal as possible and try not to get overwhelmed with the studio, the team or the mechanics.

- And finally: when I worked in radio this sign was sitting in the studio: 'Smile – everyone can hear it'.

Being part of a panel interview

There is a chance you will be on media discussing a topic with other people in a more heated way as part of a panel discussion. As well as everything we have looked at so far, there are some other things to be aware of in this situation.

- If you can't properly answer a question, then tell the interviewer you will find out and get back to them by the end of the show (make sure you always do).

- If an interviewer or another person on the panel is pursuing or harassing you, stay at the same emotional level throughout. No matter how much they interrupt you, don't get angry. Keep your voice at the same level no matter who else raises theirs. Don't get into a vocal competition – especially men with women.

- Remember to answer the data part of the question, not the emotional part.

- If you are on TV or radio and the discussion is getting abusive in any way then say 'I have a lot to offer but if you don't give me the chance I will leave'.

- If you are on a panel discussion and you wish to interrupt, an interruption starts physically, not verbally: sit up straight, lean forward, raise your hand and try to get the interviewer's attention first.

- You need to know the names of everyone on the panel and any callers or audience members who ask a question. When you do interrupt verbally you need to use the person's name whom you are interrupting.

- If you are sitting at a table as part of a panel, sit up straight and really claim the space. Don't make yourself small or put your hands under the desk.

- A floor manager is in charge in a TV studio. Watch them at all times and you will get a good sense of what is going on.

What do I wear on television?

This is the number one question I get asked when people come to me for media training. It is a very important question and, indeed, a very important outfit. Here are 20 tips on how to dress for television:

1. The camera does add 10 pounds, so you will look bigger on television than you are in real life.

2. Man or woman, you must wear make up on television otherwise you look washed out.

3. If you are going on TV there will be a make-up artist who will powder you (if you are a man) and make you up (if you are a woman).

4. Choose a hairstyle that emphasises your face and doesn't hide it.

5. You should dress for television in a way that isn't going to take away from your messages.

6. Wear clothes that are comfortable and that you won't be pulling at in any way.

7. If you are a woman wearing a shirt, make sure that when you sit down the shirt does not gape. Use double-sided sticky tape to secure it if necessary.

8. White reflects light and black absorbs it so they are not the best colours to wear on television. Good colours are navy, chocolate and charcoal for suits, and bright colours look great on TV (not pastels).

9. Some studios have what is called a 'green/blue screen'. If that is the case, if you wear anything green or blue you will blend into the set. Check with the show if they use one of these, or, if in doubt, bring a second clothing option. In fact, I suggest you always bring a second option of clothing with you.

10. Do not choose jewellery that will make a noise and be too distracting. Also, don't wear any badges, ribbons or anything that will allow someone to make a judgement about you – unless that is your goal.

11. When dressing for television you are best to choose spring/autumn clothes rather than winter/summer clothes.

12. If you want to look like a professional, wear a tailored jacket.

13. Be careful with polka dots or any kind of check pattern as they dance on camera.

14. Men can make a statement with the tie they choose to wear – make sure it is the right statement though.

15. Wearing glasses is not a problem as long as the rim is not too thick; the audience must be able to see your eyes as they are essential for communication.

16. Be very careful of having something written on your clothes – the audience at home will spend the entire time trying to read it.

17. If you are someone who perspires a lot, buy a deodorant product like Mitchum (any good chemist will have it), or buy sweat protector pads and sew them into your shirts.

18. Women, be careful of how much leg or cleavage you show.

19. If you are a woman who blushes, make sure you are wearing a high-neck top or scarf.

20. Be wary of wearing the latest trends, as in two months' time you may look dated.

Before the interview	✓
Find out the duration/time/location of the interview	
Confirm the topic/content/background to the interview	
Research the style of the programme and the presenter	
Have a bag of great things to say	
Prepare likely questions and answers	
Prepare your notes	
Plan your wardrobe	

On the day of the interview	✓
Check the daily papers for any relevant breaking stories	
Revise notes and rehearse your messages	
Make sure you arrive 30 minutes early	
Be aware of your surroundings – you are **ON** the moment you enter the studio	
Get control of your nerves	
Don't tamper with the set in any way	
Ensure you have water with you at all times	
Look at the presenter, not the camera (for TV)	

▶

On the day of the interview	✓
Stay seated until you are told to move by a floor manager or producer	
Thank the presenter	
There is no 'off the record' – don't get too comfortable with the presenter	

After the interview	✓
Contact the producer/researcher to thank them	
Request a copy of the interview for review	
Listen back to the interview in full	

Chapter cheat sheet

Generally, a TV or radio show will have:

- a presenter;
- a producer;
- a researcher;
- a runner.

You must prepare three things for a media interview:

1. The key points you want the listener to remember.
2. How to make those points interesting and understandable for the listener.
3. The kind of questions you are likely to be asked and how best to answer them.

Interviews can happen in many different ways:

- pre-recorded interviews;
- live over the phone;
- live in a radio studio;
- live in a TV studio.

The presenter of the show is not the audience you are talking to.

The presenter is just a telephone through which to talk to the audience.

ONE DAY AT A TIME

Keep improving your communication

At the beginning of my career, and for a long time after, I believed success was something that happened in a straight line. I believed success was like climbing a ladder.

I believed if I worked very hard I would reach my point of success. Once I reached my definition and destination of success I could stop trying.

Up to that point I was focused, I had passion, I came up with ideas and I persisted until my moment of success came. Because of this effort and commitment I reached the top of my chosen ladder.

Once there, filled with pride and achievement, I stopped.

I stopped working hard, I stopped being focused, I stopped being creative and I stopped being persistent.

I gave myself a big pat on the back and I stopped.

You can probably guess what happened next. Within two years or so, without any warning or concern for its effect on me, my success disappeared. Gone, like water running through my fingers.

By the time I realised what was happening it was too late to salvage all I had worked so hard for. Without notification or consideration, it vanished. Poof!

This was one of the hardest lessons I had to learn in my working life and it took me a long time to understand what happened, admit to my failings, dust myself off and try again.

Success is not a ladder you climb, where once you get what you want you stop trying. The determination, decisions and desire that got you to your moment of success require the same energy that you will need to maintain that success.

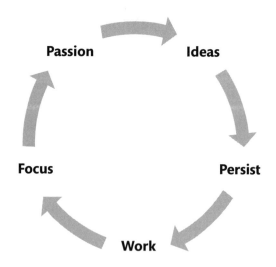

Success is not a ladder, as I once believed. Success is a circle. Success is a series of behaviours you act out every single day to reach your point of success and you must continue these, or slightly adapt them, to maintain your success.

One day at a time

So what do my life lessons have to do with you?

It can be very easy to nail a networking event, have a fabulous feedback session or, indeed, even do a marvellous media interview and believe you have mastered the art of communication.

The ability to be a great verbal communicator is not an end destination at the top of a ladder. It is not something you can take for granted once you have reached a certain stage in your career or had some success at it.

Successful communication is a skill that requires continuous commitment and effort.

In order to achieve success in your verbal communication skills, you will have to commit to keep improving those skills every day.

There are three elements you must aspire to work on every day: preparation, experience and feedback.

Let's look at each one.

Preparation

Ninety per cent of the success of your communication in all the scenarios we have explored in this book come down to preparation.

I wish I could give you a simpler, sexier or more effortless path, but I can't.

I don't have a magic formula that allows you to deliver brilliant verbal communication without knowing the purpose, understanding the listener and preparing to speak.

Each situation you face every day will be different. Each human being will be individual and even when you interact with the same people regularly, they will think, know and feel differently today than they did yesterday.

No matter how confident you feel, no matter how well another exchange went last week, no matter how experienced you are, you must treat each interaction as a new one. You must stop, think and prepare using the approach and templates in this book every time you communicate.

Fail to **Prepare**
Prepare to **Fail**

Experience

Communication is a skill. To build a skill you need to do it as much as possible so you can learn.

As you learn any new skill you go through **four stages of learning**. This learning process is about making mistakes and learning from those mistakes. However, when we make mistakes as an adult we judge ourselves harshly for 'not doing it right', 'not being good enough', and we tell our selves 'I can never learn this'.

Ironically, not doing it right and making mistakes as you learn to communicate are vital steps in the learning process to gain this great skill. To become a great communicator you have to go through the four stages of learning, as uncovered by Abraham Maslow in 1943 in his 'A Theory of Human Motivation', *Psychological Review* 50(4):

1. **Unconscious incompetence:** 'I don't know that I don't know how to do this.' This is the stage of blissful ignorance before learning begins.

2. **Conscious incompetence:** 'I know that I don't know how to do this.'

This is the most difficult stage, where learning begins and where you will start judging yourself harshly. This is also the stage when most people give up. Mistakes are integral to the learning process. They're necessary because learning is essentially experimental and experience-based – trial and error. You can only learn by doing and making mistakes.

3. **Conscious competence:** 'I know I can do this. I am learning and it is showing.' As you practise more and more, you move into the third stage of learning: conscious competence. This feels better, but your communication still isn't going to be very smooth or fluid – at least not as much as you would like it to be. You will still have to think a lot about your behaviours.

4. **Unconscious competence:** 'I'm a natural!' This is the final stage of learning a skill, and when it has become a natural part of us – although you still need to prepare before each interaction.

One of the biggest challenges you may face with some of the scenarios in this book is getting the chance to do them enough to move through these four stages.

If you only give feedback twice a year you will inevitably feel stuck at the stage where you know you are not quite doing it right but you are not getting the experience to improve.

I don't know what you do for a living or how gaining this experience will look for you, but if you wish to improve you need to get as much practice and experience as possible at the communication scenario you wish to master.

Feedback

The final behaviour that is vital for your continual success is seeking feedback after you communicate.

The '70/20/10 Model in Learning and Development' was developed by Morgan McCall and his colleagues, Michael M. Lombardo and Robert W. Eichinger, at the Centre for Creative Leadership in the year 1996. It stresses the need to extend learning beyond the parameters of the classroom. It also provides a framework for improving and extending traditional training and learning into the workplace, where:

- About 70 per cent of learning comes from direct experience of the skill through workplace learning and performance support.

- About 20 per cent of learning comes from social learning and feedback from mentors or managers.

- About 10 per cent of learning comes from structured courses and reading.

TO DEVELOP GREAT COMMUNICATION SKILLS YOU MUST:

- understand and gain the skill through attending courses and reading books;
- communicate on the job (or wherever possible) on a regular basis;
- receive feedback on a continual basis in relation to your communication.

In an earlier chapter of this book we looked at the importance of giving and receiving feedback in order to highlight any strengths or weaknesses that may not be visible to us because they are in our blind spot.

Asking for feedback and getting it is vital for your continuous improvement. If you go to a job interview and you don't get the job, ask for feedback. If you run a workshop, ask for feedback at the end of the day. If you do a media interview on radio, listen back to it yourself as well as asking for feedback.

Conclusion

We live in a world full of options and choices, especially when it comes to communication. We can easily send an email, make a phone call or connect on social media.

All of these are legitimate forms of communication that can be very useful and appropriate at the right time. However, in the hierarchy of communication a face-to-face exchange will maximise your ability to connect on an emotional level. You can look into someone's eyes, pick up on non-verbal cues and offer an appropriate response in every situation.

Face-to-face verbal communication is the most efficient form of communication. A recent Harvard/Columbia study showed a 38 per cent increase in retention with face-to-face meetings. Face to face is desirable for creating new relationships, renewing old relationships, communicating bad news and for resolving conflicts.

Being able to communicate well verbally is not the sole answer to all business challenges, but it is a vital skill to help you succeed in your chosen career path, behave authentically and build lasting business relationships.

Good luck out there.

INDEX